Recommendations for Linkword

'I am happy to say that I was delighted, and very impressed with your course'
Paul Daniels

'We have found the Linkword programmes to be both effective and entertaining'
Brian Ablett, Training Development Office, British Caledonian

'The most entertaining language tutor of all: it works and it's fun'
Jack Schofield, The Guardian

'Feel free to quote me as a satisfied customer'
Michael Woodhall, Director Language Learning Centre, Manchester Business School

'It took 12 hours to teach a regime that normally takes 40 hours'
Peter Marsh, Thomson Holidays

'I was quite frankly astounded at how effective this visual imagery was as an aid to memory retention'
Lolita Taylor, Popular Computer World

'I tried the system out in German and French and was amazed at how quickly it worked'
Jan McCann, Toronto Sun

COURSE DESIGNER AND WRITER

Dr Michael M. Gruneberg, designer and writer of the Gruneberg Linkword Language Courses, is Senior Lecturer in Psychology at University College, Swansea, Wales. He has published a number of well-known books on memory, and is an organiser of two major international conferences on Practical Aspects of Memory. He has also published a number of research papers concerned with practical and theoretical aspects of memory. For the past few years he has worked with a number of linguists in designing the Gruneberg Linkword Language System.

LANGUAGE CONSULTANT

Brian Cainen, B.A., is Lecturer in Romance Studies, University College of Swansea, Wales.

Also available from Corgi Books:

LINKWORD LANGUAGE SYSTEM – FRENCH
LINKWORD LANGUAGE SYSTEM – SPANISH
LINKWORD LANGUAGE SYSTEM – GERMAN

Italian

Michael M. Gruneberg

Language Consultant
Brian Cainen

CORGI BOOKS

To John Beloff

LINKWORD LANGUAGE SYSTEM – ITALIAN

A CORGI BOOK 0 552 13056 7

First publication in Great Britain

PRINTING HISTORY
Corgi edition published 1987

Copyright © Dr Michael Gruneberg 1987

This book is set in 9/10 pt Century
by Colset Private Limited, Singapore.

Corgi Books are published by Transworld Publishers
Ltd., 61 – 63 Uxbridge Road, Ealing, London W5 5SA,
in Australia by Transworld Publishers (Australia)
Pty. Ltd., 15 – 23 Helles Avenue, Moorebank, NSW
2170, and in New Zealand by Transworld Publishers
(N.Z.) Ltd., Cnr. Moselle and Waipareira Avenues,
Henderson, Auckland.

Printed and bound in Great Britain
by The Guernsey Press Co. Ltd., Guernsey, Channel Islands.

Contents

A Foreword by Paul Daniels

As you may know I, Paul Daniels, am a professional magician, and as such am involved in the business of deception. I am also writing this foreword without ever having seen the full text of this book.

Add these two facts together and you may well wonder why or how I can speak with any degree of authority or expect to be believed when I extol the virtues of the Linkword system.

Well, the simple truth is that one Monday morning at nine a.m. I did not speak a single word of Spanish and by five p.m. on the following Friday I knew hundreds of words of Spanish! I know that is true because I counted them!! Please note the use of the word 'knew' in the last sentence . . . it was chosen deliberately . . . I knew the words positively enough to KNOW that when I said them they were the correct words. My brain reeled with the excitement of learning so much so fast. At forty-eight years of age I had finally got to the stage of being able to communicate with people of another language . . . and how they loved me for trying.

A few weeks later, with no more lessons other than my own reading of Spanish newspapers and books I went on stage and performed my act entirely in Spanish, and now I am 'all fired up' and anxious to learn more. It's wonderful.

Memory systems go back a long way, and I have read many that have suggested their methods could be applied to language learning, but this system is the first I have come across where someone has actually provided a complete system that is 'ready to go'. When you first read memory systems that use idiotic association as a memory aid it is very easy to think that the idea itself is stupid, BUT IT WORKS!!!

So, do yourself a favour and don't knock it till you have tried it. Once you have found out for yourself how to use your own imagination fully to really 'see' the mental images I am sure that like me you will be wondering why this 'game' of learning language is not taught in all our schools.

Paul Daniels

Linkword Language System
– Italian

TEST YOURSELF WITH LINKWORD

Picture each of these images in your mind's eye for about 10 seconds.

○ The French for TABLECLOTH is NAPPE
  Imagine having a *NAP* on a *TABLECLOTH*.

○ The German for GENTLEMEN is HERREN
  Imagine a *HERRING* dangling from the door of a *GENTLEMEN'S* toilet.

○ The Italian for FLY is MOSCA.
  Imagine *FLIES* invading *MOSCOW*.

○ The Spanish for SUITCASE is MALETA
  Imagine *MY LETTER* in your *SUITCASE*.

○ The French for HEDGEHOG is HERISSON.
  Imagine your *HAIRY SON* looks like a *HEDGEHOG*.

○ The German for LETTER is BRIEF.
  Imagine a *BRIEF LETTER*.

○ The Italian for DRAWER is CASSETTO.
  Imagine you keep *CASSETTES* in a *DRAWER*.

○ The Spanish for WAITRESS is CAMARERA.
  Imagine a *WAITRESS* with a *CAMERA* slung around her neck!

NOW TURN OVER

○ What is the English for CAMARERA? _____

○ What is the English for CASSETTO? _____

○ What is the English for BRIEF? _____

○ What is the English for HERISSON? _____

○ What is the English for MALETA? _____

○ What is the English for MOSCA? _____

○ What is the English for HERREN? _____

○ What is the English for NAPPE? _____

TURN BACK FOR THE ANSWERS

Do not expect to get them all correct at the first attempt. However, if you feel you got more right than you normally would have — then this course will suit you!

INTRODUCTION

Who is Linkword for?

The short answer is that Linkword is for anyone and everyone who wants to learn the basics of a language in a hurry. Linkword is for the holidaymaker, for the business person, for school work or for pleasure. It can be used by children or by adults. Even young children who cannot read can be taught Italian words by a parent reading out the images.

How to Use Linkword

1] LEARNING THE WHOLE COURSE (WORDS AND GRAMMAR)

The Linkword Courses have been carefully designed to teach you a basic grammar and words in a simple step by step way that anyone can follow. After about 10—12 hours or even less, you will have a vocabulary of 350—400 words and the ability to string these words together to form sentences. The course is ideal, therefore, for the holidaymaker or business person who just wants the basics in a hurry so he or she can be understood, e.g. in the hotel, arriving at their destination, sightseeing, shopping, eating out, in emergencies, telling the time and so on.

2] LEARNING THE WORDS ONLY

If you are revising for exams and just want to boost your vocabulary, or if you are going abroad and just want to learn some words so that you can cope with emergencies say, or order a meal in a restaurant etc., then just look up the Table of Contents on page v and turn to the section you want. You can read only the pages with the words and images. You should, however test yourself to make sure that the words are "sticking".

Obviously if you only learn the words you will not be able to communicate as well as if you learn both words and grammar. However you *can* often communicate using just one word, e.g. "bill!" will communicate to the waiter that you want the bill!

One word of warning however. The words will not stick as well in your memory if they are learned as single words compared to being learned with grammar as part of the whole course.

4

Instructions

1] You will be presented with words like this:
The Italian for HAND is MANO
Imagine a MAN warming his HAND.
What you do is to imagine this picture in your mind's eye as vividly as possible.

2] After you have read the image you should think about it in your mind's eye for about 10 seconds before moving on to the next word. If you do not spend enough time thinking about the image it will not stick in your memory as well as it should.

3] Sometimes the word in Italian and in English is the same or very similar. For example, the Italian for "taxi" is "taxi". When this happens you will be asked to associate the word in some way with spaghetti.

Imagine a taxi with spaghetti on the seat.

Whenever spaghetti comes to mind, therefore, you will know the word is the same or similar in both English and Italian.

4] It is very important to realise that some groups of words are more difficult to learn than others. If you find this do not worry, just go on on to the next set of words and forget you have had any difficulty. The important thing to appreciate is how much you *do* learn very quickly.

5] The examples given in the course may well strike you as silly and bizarre. They have deliberately been given in this way to show up points of grammar and to get away from the idea that you should remember useful phrases "parrot fashion".

6] ACCENTS
In this course accents will be written like this SI' when the word is in capitals and like this sì when the word is not in capitals.

7] PRONUNCIATION
The approximate pronunciation of words is given in brackets after the word is presented for the first time.
For example: The Italian for COW is MUCCA (MOOKKA)
            (MOOKKA) is the way the word is pronounced.

Do not worry too much about pronunciation to begin with. The approximate pronunciation given in brackets will allow you to be understood. If you would like to listen to the exact pronunciation, an audio-tape containing all the words on the course is available from Corgi Books.

Important Note
The first section of the course can basically be regarded as a training section designed to get you into the Linkword method quickly and easily. After about 45 minutes you will have a vocabulary of about 30 words and you will be able to translate sentences. Once you have finished Section I you will have the confidence to go through the rest of the course just as quickly. Animal words are used in the first section as they are a large group of "easy to image" words. Many animal words of course are useful to have as they are often met abroad e.g. dog, cat, etc., or they are edible!

Finally ...
When it comes to translating sentences the answers are given at the foot of the page. You may find it useful to cover up the answers before you tackle the translations.

Section 1   ANIMALS

N.B. The word on the right-hand side of the page (IN BRACKETS) is the way the word is pronounced.

THINK OF EACH IMAGE IN YOUR MIND'S EYE FOR ABOUT TEN SECONDS

○ The Italian for CAT is GATTO   (GATTO)
   Imagine you've GOT TO hold a cat.

○ The Italian for BIRD is UCCELLO   (OOCHELLO)
   Imagine telling a bird in an animal orchestra
   "YOU CELLO, me conductor".

○ The Italian for GOAT is CAPRA   (KAPRA)
   Imagine a goat looking up at night at the
   constellation CAPRICORN.

○ The Italian for BULL is TORO   (TORO)
   Imagine a TOREADOR fighting a bull.

○ The Italian for COW is MUCCA   (MOOKKA)
   Imagine a cow going Moo — a MOO-COW.

○ The Italian for DUCK is ANITRA   (ANEETRA)
   Imagine a duck walking along a high wire —
   A NEAT TRick.

○ The Italian for GOOSE is OCA   (OKA)
   Imagine a goose shouting O.K! O.K!

○ The Italian for PIG is PORCO   (PORKO)
   Imagine eating PORK straight from a pig.

○ The Italian for DONKEY is ASINO   (AZEENO)
   Imagine a donkey looking like an ASS I KNOW.

○ The Italian for FROG is RANA   (RANA)
   Imagine you RAN A mile after seeing a
   horrible frog.

YOU CAN WRITE YOUR ANSWERS IN

○ What is the English for rana?   _____

○ What is the English for asino?   _____

○ What is the English for porco?   _____

○ What is the English for oca?   _____

○ What is the English for anitra?   _____

○ What is the English for mucca?   _____

○ What is the English for toro?   _____

○ What is the English for capra?   _____

○ What is the English for uccello?   _____

○ What is the English for gatto?   _____

TURN BACK FOR THE ANSWERS

○ What is the Italian for frog? _____

○ What is the Italian for donkey? _____

○ What is the Italian for pig? _____

○ What is the Italian for goose? _____

○ What is the Italian for duck? _____

○ What is the Italian for cow? _____

○ What is the Italian for bull? _____

○ What is the Italian for goat? _____

○ What is the Italian for bird? _____

○ What is the Italian for cat? _____

TURN BACK FOR THE ANSWERS

ELEMENTARY GRAMMAR

In Italian all nouns, or things, are either MASCULINE or FEMININE.

If they end in an "o" they are masculine.

For example, the Italian for BIRD (UCCELLO) and for cat (GATTO) end in "o" and are therefore masculine words.

If the word ends in an "a" it is a feminine word. So, MUCCA for COW, and OCA for GOOSE are feminine words.

Now cover up the answers below and translate the following:

What are the genders of:

(You can write your answers in)

PORCO
ASINO
RANA
CAPRA

The answers are:

PORCO is MASCULINE
ASINO is MASCULINE
RANA is FEMININE
CAPRA is FEMININE

Some words do not end in "o" or "a".

Do not worry about these words, we will deal with them later.

MORE ANIMALS

THINK OF EACH IMAGE IN YOUR MIND'S EYE FOR ABOUT TEN SECONDS

○ The Italian for RAT is TOPO   (TOPO)
   Imagine a rat on TOP O' a pole.

○ The Italian for WASP is VESPA   (VESPA)
   Imagine a wasp making a sound like a
   WHISPER in your ear.

○ The Italian for TROUT is TROTA   (TROTA)
   Imagine a trout eating a pig's TROTTER.

○ The Italian for DOG is CANE   (KANAY)
   Imagine a dog chasing a CANARY.

○ The Italian for FISH is PESCE   (PAYSHAY)
   Imagine a PATIENT in hospital being fed a
   diet of fish.

○ The Italian for BEAR is ORSO   (ORSO)
   Imagine a bear clinging to a HORSE OH!

○ The Italian for OYSTER is OSTRICA   (OSTREEKA)
   Imagine OSTRICHES eating oysters.

○ The Italian for BUTTERFLY is FARFALLA   (FARFALLA)
   Imagine saying to a young boy who is good at
   catching butterflies "You will go FAR, FELLOW!"

○ The Italian for CATERPILLAR is BRUCO   (BROOKO)
   Imagine throwing caterpillars into a BROOK OH!

○ The Italian for INSECT is INSETTO   (EENSETTO)
   Imagine INSECTS crawling over a plate of
   spaghetti.

15

YOU CAN WRITE YOUR ANSWERS IN

○ What is the English for insetto?   _____

○ What is the English for bruco?   _____

○ What is the English for farfalla?   _____

○ What is the English for ostrica?   _____

○ What is the English for orso?   _____

○ What is the English for pesce?   _____

○ What is the English for cane?   _____

○ What is the English for trota?   _____

○ What is the English for vespa?   _____

○ What is the English for topo?   _____

TURN BACK FOR THE ANSWERS

○ What is the Italian for insect? _____

○ What is the Italian for caterpillar? _____

○ What is the Italian for butterfly? _____

○ What is the Italian for oyster? _____

○ What is the Italian for bear? _____

○ What is the Italian for fish? _____

○ What is the Italian for dog? _____

○ What is the Italian for trout? _____

○ What is the Italian for wasp? _____

○ What is the Italian for rat? _____

TURN BACK FOR THE ANSWERS

ELEMENTARY GRAMMAR

You learned after the last group of words that all nouns are either masculine or feminine. If they end in "o" they are masculine, like TORO for BULL. If they end in "a" they are feminine, like CAPRA for GOAT.

If they do not end in either an "o" or an "a" you can assume that they are masculine, although you will make the occasional mistake. Where there are exceptions in this course, we will tell you.

If the word is masculine, then the word for THE is IL (pronounced EEL).

So,

    IL TORO   is THE BULL

    IL GATTO is THE CAT

    IL TOPO   is THE RAT

(Imagine a man eating EELs!)

If the word is feminine, the word for THE is LA.

So,

    LA RANA   is THE FROG

    LA MUCCA is THE COW

    LA VESPA is THE WASP

As was said just now, if the word does not end in "o" or "a", you can assume it is masculine.

So,

    IL CANE   is THE DOG

    IL PESCE is THE FISH

Now cover up the answers below and translate the following:

(You can write your answers in)

1. THE CAT
2. THE GOAT
3. THE BULL
4. THE FROG
5. THE RAT
6. THE DOG
7. THE FISH
8. THE BUTTERFLY

The answers are:

1. IL GATTO
2. LA CAPRA
3. IL TORO
4. LA RANA
5. IL TOPO
6. IL CANE
7. IL PESCE
8. LA FARFALLA

SOME MORE GRAMMAR

If a word begins with a vowel, then THE is always L' — no matter what the gender.

So,

L'UCCELLO is THE BIRD

L'ORSO is THE BEAR

L'OCA is THE GOOSE

L'ANITRA is THE DUCK

L'INSETTO is THE INSECT

To summarise:

IL is MASCULINE

LA is FEMININE

If the word starts with a vowel, then THE is L' — whether masculine or feminine.

ADJECTIVES — DESCRIPTION WORDS

THINK OF EACH IMAGE IN YOUR MIND'S EYE FOR ABOUT TEN SECONDS

○ The Italian for QUICK is RAPIDO   (RAPEEDO)
Imagine being QUICK and RAPID.

○ The Italian for QUIET is   (TRANKWEELLO)
TRANQUILLO
Imagine being QUIET and TRANQUIL.

○ The Italian for HARD is DURO   (DOORO)
Imagine something HARD and DURABLE.

○ The Italian for FRESH is FRESCO   (FRESKO)
Imagine seeing a FRESCO FRESHLY
painted on a wall.

○ The Italian for BAD is CATTIVO   (KATTEEVO)
Imagine a BAD cat — a CAT-EVIL.

○ The Italian for EMPTY is VUOTO   (VWOTO)
Imagine that you EMPTY WATER from
the bath.

○ The Italian for FULL is PIENO   (PYAYNO)
Imagine you are so FULL, you have to
sit on a PIANO.

○ The Italian for TIRED is STANCO   (STANKO)
Imagine someone who was dead TIRED,
STANK O' drink.

○ The Italian for SMALL is PICCOLO   (PEEKKOLO)
Imagine a very SMALL boy playing a
PICCOLO.

○ The Italian for EXPENSIVE is CARO   (KARO)
Imagine an EXPENSIVE CAR.

YOU CAN WRITE YOUR ANSWERS IN

○ What is the English for caro?　　　　＿＿＿＿＿＿＿

○ What is the English for piccolo?　　＿＿＿＿＿＿＿

○ What is the English for stanco?　　 ＿＿＿＿＿＿＿

○ What is the English for pieno?　　　＿＿＿＿＿＿＿

○ What is the English for vuoto?　　　＿＿＿＿＿＿＿

○ What is the English for cattivo?　　 ＿＿＿＿＿＿＿

○ What is the English for fresco?　　　＿＿＿＿＿＿＿

○ What is the English for duro?　　　 ＿＿＿＿＿＿＿

○ What is the English for tranquillo?　＿＿＿＿＿＿＿

○ What is the English for rapido?　　　＿＿＿＿＿＿＿

TURN BACK FOR THE ANSWERS

○ What is the Italian for expensive?   _____

○ What is the Italian for small?   _____

○ What is the Italian for tired?   _____

○ What is the Italian for full?   _____

○ What is the Italian for empty?   _____

○ What is the Italian for bad?   _____

○ What is the Italian for fresh?   _____

○ What is the Italian for hard?   _____

○ What is the Italian for quiet?   _____

○ What is the Italian for quick?   _____

TURN BACK FOR THE ANSWERS

ELEMENTARY GRAMMAR
The Italian word for IS is E' (pronounced as the E in HEN).

So,

    THE CAT IS QUICK is IL GATTO E' RAPIDO
    THE RAT IS QUICK is IL TOPO E' RAPIDO

If the noun is feminine, such as LA RANA for FROG, or LA MUCCA for COW, then the ending of the adjective changes to an "a" from an "o" to agree with the word.

If the noun is masculine, the adjective ends in "o".

So, to summarise,

    THE COW IS QUICK   is LA MUCCA E' RAPIDA
    THE BULL IS QUICK is IL TORO E' RAPIDO

Now cover up the answers below and translate the following:

(You can write your answers in)

1. THE BULL IS TIRED
2. THE BIRD IS EXPENSIVE
3. THE FROG IS QUIET
4. THE FISH IS FRESH
5. THE DONKEY IS BAD

The answers are:

1. IL TORO E' STANCO
2. L'UCCELLO E' CARO
3. LA RANA E' TRANQUILLA
4. IL PESCE E' FRESCO
5. L'ASINO E' CATTIVO

Now cover up the answers below and translate the following:

(You can write your answers in)

1. L'ANITRA E' CARA
2. IL BRUCO E' STANCO
3. IL CANE E' PIENO
4. L'INSETTO E' CATTIVO
5. IL PORCO E' TRANQUILLO

The answers are:

1. THE DUCK IS EXPENSIVE
2. THE CATERPILLAR IS TIRED
3. THE DOG IS FULL
4. THE INSECT IS BAD
5. THE PIG IS QUIET

SOME USEFUL ANIMAL WORDS

THINK OF EACH IMAGE IN YOUR MIND'S EYE FOR ABOUT TEN SECONDS

○ The Italian for BEE is APE   (APAY)
  Imagine a bee stinging AN APE, or imagine
  a HAPPY bee.
  (N.B. APE is a feminine word)

○ The Italian for HORSE is CAVALLO   (KAVALLO)
  Imagine horses in the CAVALRY.

○ The Italian for JELLYFISH is MEDUSA   (MEDOOZA)
  Imagine seeing what looks like a jellyfish in
  the water, but when you look closely it is
  MEDUSA with her head of snakes.

○ The Italian for FLY is MOSCA   (MOSKA)
  Imagine MOSCOW invaded by flies.

○ The Italian for MOSQUITO is ZANZARA   (DZANDZARA)
  Imagine being pestered by mosquitoes when
  you visit ZANZIBAR.

○ The Italian for CHICKEN is POLLO   (POLLO)
  Imagine using a chicken to play POLO
  instead of a ball.

○ The Italian for SHEEP is PECORA   (PEKORA)
  Imagine a girl asking you to PICK HER A
  sheep from the flock.

YOU CAN WRITE YOUR ANSWERS IN

○ What is the English for pecora?   _____

○ What is the English for pollo?   _____

○ What is the English for zanzara?   _____

○ What is the English for mosca?   _____

○ What is the English for medusa?   _____

○ What is the English for cavallo?   _____

○ What is the English for ape?   _____

TURN BACK FOR THE ANSWERS

COVER UP THE LEFT HAND PAGE BEFORE ANSWERING

○ What is the Italian for sheep? _____

○ What is the Italian for chicken? _____

○ What is the Italian for mosquito? _____

○ What is the Italian for fly? _____

○ What is the Italian for jellyfish? _____

○ What is the Italian for horse? _____

○ What is the Italian for bee? _____

TURN BACK FOR THE ANSWERS

ELEMENTARY GRAMMAR
When you have a noun and an adjective together like HARD PIG, FRESH FISH, then the adjective usually comes after the noun.

So,

THE HARD PIG   is   IL PORCO DURO

THE FRESH FISH   is   IL PESCE FRESCO

THE BAD MOSQUITO is   LA ZANZARA CATTIVA

Now cover up the answers below and translate the following:

(You can write your answers in)

1. THE QUICK HORSE IS QUIET
2. THE TIRED FLY IS BAD
3. THE EXPENSIVE BIRD IS FULL
4. THE SMALL BEE IS EMPTY
5. THE HARD CHICKEN IS BAD

The answers are:

1. IL CAVALLO RAPIDO E' TRANQUILLO
2. LA MOSCA STANCA E' CATTIVA
3. L'UCCELLO CARO E' PIENO
4. L'APE PICCOLA E' VUOTA
5. IL POLLO DURO E' CATTIVO

Now cover up the answers below and translate the following:

(You can write your answers in)

1. LA MUCCA CATTIVA E' PICCOLA
2. L'ORSO RAPIDO E' CARO
3. IL TOPO FRESCO E' PIENO
4. LA VESPA DURA E' VUOTA
5. LA TROTA TRANQUILLA E' STANCA

The answers are:

1. THE BAD COW IS SMALL
2. THE QUICK BEAR IS EXPENSIVE
3. THE FRESH RAT IS FULL
4. THE HARD WASP IS EMPTY
5. THE QUIET TROUT IS TIRED

IMPORTANT NOTE
Some of the sentences in this course might strike you as being a bit odd!

However, they have been carefully constructed to make you think much more about what you are translating. This helps the memory process and gets away from the idea of learning useful phrases "parrot fashion".

But of course, having learned with the help of these seemingly odd sentences, you can easily construct your own sentences to suit your particular needs.

Section 2   HOTEL/HOME, FURNITURE, COLOURS

THINK OF EACH IMAGE IN YOUR MIND'S EYE FOR ABOUT TEN SECONDS

○ The Italian for BED is LETTO   (LETTO)
   Imagine a LETTER lying on your bed.

○ The Italian for TABLE is TAVOLA   (TAVOLA)
   Imagine wanting TO HAVE ALL THE
   tables together.

○ The Italian for CHAIR is SEDIA   (SAYDYA)
   Imagine a German who SAID, "YA, you
   can sit on a chair."

○ The Italian for CURTAIN is TENDA   (TENDA)
   Imagine rubbing a TENDER part of
   your leg with a curtain.

○ The Italian for CUSHION is CUSCINO   (KOOSHEENO)
   Imagine a CUSHION all covered in
   spaghetti.

○ The Italian for CUPBOARD is ARMADIO   (ARMADYO)
   Imagine boats in the Spanish ARMADA
   being loaded with cupboards.

○ The Italian for DRAWER is CASSETTO   (KASSETTO)
   Imagine putting your collection of
   CASSETTES in a drawer.

○ The Italian for MIRROR is SPECCHIO   (SPEKKYO)
   Imagine looking at the SPECKS YOU
   see on a mirror.

○ The Italian for PIANO is PIANOFORTE   (PYANOFORTAY)
   Imagine a PIANOFORTE all covered
   with spaghetti.

○ The Italian for CARPET is TAPPETO   (TAPPAYTO)
   Imagine having a shoe and being told to
   TAP IT TO music on the carpet.

YOU CAN WRITE YOUR ANSWERS IN

○ What is the English for tappeto? _____

○ What is the English for pianoforte? _____

○ What is the English for specchio? _____

○ What is the English for cassetto? _____

○ What is the English for armadio? _____

○ What is the English for cuscino? _____

○ What is the English for tenda? _____

○ What is the English for sedia? _____

○ What is the English for tavola? _____

○ What is the English for letto? _____

TURN BACK FOR THE ANSWERS

○ What is the Italian for carpet?   _____

○ What is the Italian for piano?   _____

○ What is the Italian for mirror?   _____

○ What is the Italian for drawer?   _____

○ What is the Italian for cupboard?   _____

○ What is the Italian for cushion?   _____

○ What is the Italian for curtain?   _____

○ What is the Italian for chair?   _____

○ What is the Italian for table?   _____

○ What is the Italian for bed?   _____

TURN BACK FOR THE ANSWERS

ELEMENTARY GRAMMAR

There is one further point to remember about the word THE.

You will remember that THE is IL when the noun is masculine (for example IL GATTO); it is LA if the noun is feminine (for example, LA MUCCA); and if the word starts with a vowel — for example, APE — then the word THE is L' (for example, L'APE).

NOW, finally, if a masculine word starts with an "S" and the second letter is NOT a vowel (for example, SPECCHIO), then the word for THE is LO.

So,

THE MIRROR is LO SPECCHIO

Please do not worry about this. If you made a mistake you would still be understood, and such words are not frequent.

PARTS OF THE HOUSE

THINK OF EACH IMAGE IN YOUR MIND'S EYE FOR ABOUT TEN SECONDS

○ The Italian for STAIRCASE is SCALA   (SKALA)
   Imagine SCALING stairs, two at a time.

○ The Italian for FLOOR is PAVIMENTO   (PAVEEMENTO)
   Imagine the floor of your house is used by
   everyone as a PAVEMENT.

○ The Italian for KITCHEN is CUCINA   (KOOCHEENA)
   Imagine keeping your GOOD CHINA in
   the kitchen.

○ The Italian for BEDROOM is CAMERA   (KAMAYRA)
   Imagine leaving CAMERAS all over your
   bedroom.

○ The Italian for DOOR is PORTA   (PORTA)
   Imagine a hotel PORTER who opens the
   door for you.

○ The Italian for WINDOW is FINESTRA   (FEENESTRA)
   Imagine thinking "I'll FINISH painting
   this window".

○ The Italian for ROOF is TETTO   (TETTO)
   Imagine the Edinburgh Searchlight
   TATTOO being held on your roof.

○ The Italian for ROOM is STANZA   (STANTSA)
   Imagine a man STANDS in the middle of
   a room.

○ The Italian for BATHROOM is BAGNO   (BANYO)
   Imagine they BAN YOU from using your
   bathroom.

○ The Italian for CLOAKROOM is   (GWARDAROBA)
   GUARDAROBA
   Imagine asking the attendant in a cloakroom to GUARD A ROBE which is very
   important.

YOU CAN WRITE YOUR ANSWERS IN

○ What is the English for guardaroba? _____

○ What is the English for bagno? _____

○ What is the English for stanza? _____

○ What is the English for tetto? _____

○ What is the English for finestra? _____

○ What is the English for porta? _____

○ What is the English for camera? _____

○ What is the English for cucina? _____

○ What is the English for pavimento? _____

○ What is the English for scala? _____

TURN BACK FOR THE ANSWERS

COVER UP THE LEFT HAND PAGE BEFORE ANSWERING

○ What is the Italian for cloakroom? _____

○ What is the Italian for bathroom? _____

○ What is the Italian for room? _____

○ What is the Italian for roof? _____

○ What is the Italian for window? _____

○ What is the Italian for door? _____

○ What is the Italian for bedroom? _____

○ What is the Italian for kitchen? _____

○ What is the Italian for floor? _____

○ What is the Italian for staircase? _____

TURN BACK FOR THE ANSWERS

COLOURS

**THINK OF EACH IMAGE IN YOUR MIND'S EYE FOR
ABOUT TEN SECONDS**

○ The Italian for BLACK is NERO　　　　　　(NAYRO)
Imagine the Emperor NERO dressed all in
BLACK, as he throws the Christians to the
lions.

○ The Italian for WHITE is BIANCO　　　　　(BYANKO)
Imagine your BANK ALL painted in WHITE.

○ The Italian for BLUE is BLU　　　　　　　(BLOO)
Imagine BLUE spaghetti.

○ The Italian for RED is ROSSO　　　　　　(ROSSO)
Imagine a ROSE SO RED, it is the colour of
blood.

○ The Italian for GREEN is VERDE　　　　　(VAIRDAY)
Imagine the Italian composer VERDI,
composing in an all-GREEN suit.

○ The Italian for BROWN is MARRONE　　　(MARRONAY)
Imagine a BROWN MARROW NEIGHING
like a horse when you pick it up.

○ The Italian for SILVER is ARGENTEO　　(ARJENTAYO)
Imagine sending SILVER to the
ARGENTINE.

○ The Italian for GOLDEN is D'ORO　　　　(DORO)
Imagine holding a GOLD ORE in your hands.

○ The Italian for GREY is GRIGIO　　　　　(GREEJO)
Imagine someone with a GREY face is
waiting to GREET YOU when you arrive
home.

○ The Italian for YELLOW is GIALLO　　　(JALLO)
Imagine YELLOW spaghetti.

YOU CAN WRITE YOUR ANSWERS IN

○ What is the English for giallo? _____

○ What is the English for grigio? _____

○ What is the English for d'oro? _____

○ What is the English for argenteo? _____

○ What is the English for marrone? _____

○ What is the English for verde? _____

○ What is the English for rosso? _____

○ What is the English for blu? _____

○ What is the English for bianco? _____

○ What is the English for nero? _____

TURN BACK FOR THE ANSWERS

○ What is the Italian for yellow?   _____

○ What is the Italian for grey?   _____

○ What is the Italian for golden?   _____

○ What is the Italian for silver?   _____

○ What is the Italian for brown?   _____

○ What is the Italian for green?   _____

○ What is the Italian for red?   _____

○ What is the Italian for blue?   _____

○ What is the Italian for white?   _____

○ What is the Italian for black?   _____

TURN BACK FOR THE ANSWERS

Now cover up the answers below and translate the following:

(You can write your answers in)

1. THE BLACK DRAWER IS EMPTY
2. THE FRESH CARPET IS SILVER
3. THE GOLDEN CUSHION IS FULL
4. THE WHITE PIANO IS SMALL
5. THE GREY DOOR IS HARD

The answers are:

1. IL CASSETTO NERO E' VUOTO
2. IL TAPPETO FRESCO E' ARGENTEO
3. IL CUSCINO D'ORO E' PIENO
4. IL PIANOFORTE BIANCO E' PICCOLO
5. LA PORTA GRIGIA E' DURA

Now cover up the answers below and translate the following:

(You can write your answers in)

1. LA CAMERA ROSSA E' TRANQUILLA
2. IL TETTO D'ORO E' CARO
3. LA FINESTRA PICCOLA E' GIALLA
4. LA CUCINA BIANCA E' VUOTA
5. LA SCALA NERA E' DURA

The answers are:

1. THE RED BEDROOM IS QUIET
2. THE GOLDEN ROOF IS EXPENSIVE
3. THE SMALL WINDOW IS YELLOW
4. THE WHITE KITCHEN IS EMPTY
5. THE BLACK STAIR IS HARD

SOME MORE USEFUL WORDS

THINK OF EACH IMAGE IN YOUR MIND'S EYE FOR ABOUT TEN SECONDS

○ The Italian for HIGH is ALTO   (ALTO)
Imagine being at a HIGH ALTITUDE.

○ The Italian for UGLY is BRUTTO   (BROOTTO)
Imagine looking at an UGLY BRUTE.

○ The Italian for CLEAN is PULITO   (POOLEETO)
Imagine being told PULL IT TO make it
CLEAN

○ The Italian for DIRTY is SPORCO   (SPORKO)
Imagine rubbing a DIRTY lamp until it
SPARKLES.

○ The Italian for HEAVY is PESANTE   (PAYZANTAY)
Imagine a very HEAVY Italian PEASANT.

○ The Italian LOW is BASSO   (BASSO)
Imagine a BASSOON playing a very LOW
note.

○ The Italian for DEEP is PROFONDO   (PROFOONDO)
Imagine thinking DEEP, PROFOUND
thoughts.

○ The Italian for SLOW is LENTO   (LENTO)
Imagine you do not like LENTILS, and you
are eating them very SLOWLY.

○ The Italian for NARROW is STRETTO   (STRETTO)
Imagine being on the STRAIGHT and
NARROW.

○ The Italian for WIDE is LARGO   (LARGO)
Imagine a footballer putting the ball WIDE
after drinking too much LAGER.

YOU CAN WRITE YOUR ANSWERS IN

○ What is the English for largo? _____

○ What is the English for stretto? _____

○ What is the English for lento? _____

○ What is the English for profondo? _____

○ What is the English for basso? _____

○ What is the English for pesante? _____

○ What is the English for sporco? _____

○ What is the English for pulito? _____

○ What is the English for brutto? _____

○ What is the English for alto? _____

TURN BACK FOR THE ANSWERS

○ What is the Italian for wide? _____

○ What is the Italian for narrow? _____

○ What is the Italian for slow? _____

○ What is the Italian for deep? _____

○ What is the Italian for low? _____

○ What is the Italian for heavy? _____

○ What is the Italian for dirty? _____

○ What is the Italian for clean? _____

○ What is the Italian for ugly? _____

○ What is the Italian for high? _____

TURN BACK FOR THE ANSWERS

ELEMENTARY GRAMMAR

You will remember, from the last section, that the ending of an adjective always agrees with a noun.

For example,

IL TETTO NERO   is THE BLACK ROOF

LA STANZA NERA is THE BLACK ROOM

You will probably have noticed, however, that you have just been given some adjectives which do not end in "o" or "a".

For example,

PESANTE for HEAVY

VERDE   for GREEN

When this happens you just leave the adjective alone, whatever it goes with.

For example,

THE BED IS GREEN   is IL LETTO E' VERDE

THE TABLE IS HEAVY is LA TAVOLA E' PESANTE

Now cover up the answers below and translate the following:

(You can write your answers in)

1. THE RED CHAIR IS DIRTY
2. THE BLACK FLOOR IS UGLY
3. THE YELLOW CARPET IS CLEAN
4. THE SLOW PIG IS QUIET
5. THE GREEN CURTAIN IS HEAVY

The answers are:

1. LA SEDIA ROSSA E' SPORCA
2. IL PAVIMENTO NERO E' BRUTTO
3. IL TAPPETO GIALLO E' PULITO
4. IL PORCO LENTO E' TRANQUILLO
5. LA TENDA VERDE E' PESANTE

Now cover up the answers below and translate the following:

(You can write your answers in)

1. LA STANZA BLU E' STRETTA
2. LA GUARDAROBA VERDE E' PULITA
3. IL BAGNO MARRONE E' LARGO
4. LO SPECCHIO ARGENTEO E' SPORCO
5. L'ARMADIO BLU E' VUOTO

The answers are:

1. THE BLUE ROOM IS NARROW
2. THE GREEN CLOAKROOM IS CLEAN
3. THE BROWN BATHROOM IS WIDE
4. THE SILVER MIRROR IS DIRTY
5. THE BLUE CUPBOARD IS EMPTY

Section 3　CLOTHES/FAMILY WORDS

THINK OF EACH IMAGE IN YOUR MIND'S EYE FOR ABOUT TEN SECONDS

○ The Italian for HAT is CAPPELLO　　　(KAPPELLO)
  Imagine a school CAP in the form of a top hat.

○ The Italian for SHOE is SCARPA　　　(SKARPA)
  Imagine you SCAR PA's shoes with a razor.

○ The Italian for TROUSERS is　　　(PANTALONEE)
  PANTALONI
  Imagine you are wearing baggy
  PANTALOONS for trousers.

○ The Italian for SKIRT is GONNA　　　(GONNA)
  Imagine telling your girl friend "That skirt
  is a GONNER, it has a huge tear."

○ The Italian for BLOUSE is BLUSA　　　(BLOOZA)
  Imagine wearing a BLUE blouse.

○ The Italian for SHIRT is CAMICIA　　　(KAMEECHA)
  Imagine telling someone that "I CAN
  MEET YOU in my shirt."

○ The Italian for DRESS is VESTITO　　　(VESTEETO)
  Imagine putting your VEST on over a dress.

○ The Italian for ELASTIC is ELASTICO　　　(ELASTEEKO)
  Imagine ELASTIC bands mixed in with
  your spaghetti.

○ The Italian for JACKET is GIACCA　　　(JAKKA)
  Imagine you spill spaghetti all down your
  best JACKET.

○ The Italian for BUTTON is BOTTONE　　　(BOTTONAY)
  Imagine BUTTONS cover your spaghetti.

YOU CAN WRITE YOUR ANSWERS IN

○ What is the English for bottone? _____

○ What is the English for giacca? _____

○ What is the English for elastico? _____

○ What is the English for vestito? _____

○ What is the English for camicia? _____

○ What is the English for blusa? _____

○ What is the English for gonna? _____

○ What is the English for pantaloni? _____

○ What is the English for scarpa? _____

○ What is the English for cappello? _____

TURN BACK FOR THE ANSWERS

COVER UP THE LEFT HAND PAGE BEFORE ANSWERING

○ What is the Italian for button?   _____

○ What is the Italian for jacket?   _____

○ What is the Italian for elastic?   _____

○ What is the Italian for dress?   _____

○ What is the Italian for shirt?   _____

○ What is the Italian for blouse?   _____

○ What is the Italian for skirt?   _____

○ What is the Italian for trousers?   _____

○ What is the Italian for shoe?   _____

○ What is the Italian for hat?   _____

TURN BACK FOR THE ANSWERS

USEFUL VERBS FOR SENTENCE CONSTRUCTION

THINK OF EACH IMAGE IN YOUR MIND'S EYE FOR ABOUT TEN SECONDS

○ The Italian for HAS is HA   (A)
  Imagine AH! he HAS something.

○ The Italian for WANTS is VUOLE   (VWOLAY)
  Imagine you WANT to VOLLEY a ball.

○ The Italian for EATS is MANGIA   (MANJA)
  Imagine someone who EATS the restaurant
  MANAGER.

○ The Italian for SEES is VEDE   (VAYDAY)
  Imagine you SEE a VIDEO film.

YOU CAN WRITE YOUR ANSWERS IN

○ What is the English for vede?   _____

○ What is the English for mangia?   _____

○ What is the English for vuole?   _____

○ What is the English for ha?   _____

TURN BACK FOR THE ANSWERS

○ What is the Italian for sees? _____

○ What is the Italian for eats? _____

○ What is the Italian for wants? _____

○ What is the Italian for has? _____

TURN BACK FOR THE ANSWERS

Now cover up the answers below and translate the following:

(You can write your answers in)

1. THE HEAVY DOG SEES THE BLACK DOOR
2. THE UGLY HORSE EATS THE FRESH GOOSE
3. THE SHEEP WANTS THE GREEN TABLE
4. THE RED BATHROOM HAS THE DIRTY CARPET
5. THE WHITE JELLYFISH EATS THE SLOW CHICKEN

The answers are:

1. IL CANE PESANTE VEDE LA PORTA NERA
2. IL CAVALLO BRUTTO MANGIA L'OCA FRESCA
3. LA PECORA GIALLA VUOLE LA TAVOLA VERDE
4. IL BAGNO ROSSO HA IL TAPPETO SPORCO
5. LA MEDUSA BIANCA MANGIA IL POLLO LENTO

Now cover up the answers below and translate the following:

(You can write your answers in)

1. IL LETTO DURO E' PROFONDO
2. LA SEDIA ALTA E' BRUTTA
3. LA ZANZARA NERA VEDE L'ARMADIO BASSO
4. LA RANA VERDE MANGIA L'INSETTO LENTO
5. LA TROTA D'ORO VUOLE LA MOSCA GRIGIA (Golden is always D'ORO, whether after a masculine or feminine noun.)

The answers are:

1. THE HARD BED IS DEEP
2. THE HIGH CHAIR IS UGLY
3. THE BLACK MOSQUITO SEES THE LOW CUPBOARD
4. THE GREEN FROG EATS THE SLOW INSECT
5. THE GOLDEN TROUT WANTS THE GREY FLY

FAMILY WORDS

THINK OF EACH IMAGE IN YOUR MIND'S EYE FOR ABOUT TEN SECONDS

○ The Italian for FATHER is PADRE   (PADRAY)
   Imagine your father dressed up as a PADRE.

○ The Italian for MOTHER is (LA) MADRE   (MADRAY)
   Imagine your mother being very MAD with you.

○ The Italian for BROTHER is FRATELLO   (FRATELLO)
   Imagine your brother FRATERNISING with local girls.

○ The Italian for SISTER is SORELLA   (SORELLA)
   Imagine your friend's sister is called Ella, and she is very sore at you — SORE ELLA.

○ The Italian for HUSBAND is MARITO   (MAREETO)
   Imagine you husband is MARRIED TO you.

○ The Italian for WIFE is (LA) MOGLIE   (MOLYAY)
   Imagine you have done your wife wrong, and she will MAUL YOU when you get home.

○ The Italian for GIRL is RAGAZZA   (RAGATSA)
   Imagine a whole lot of girls cheering for their team in a REGATTA.

○ The Italian for BOY is RAGAZZO   (RAGATSO)
   Imagine boys cheering at a REGATTA.

(But remember it differs from girls in ending in "o").

○ The Italian for SON is FIGLIO   (FEELYO)
   Imagine saying to your son, who has hurt himself, "Let me FEEL YOU to see if any bones are broken."

○ The Italian for DAUGHTER is FIGLIA   (FEELYA)
   Imagine saying to your daughter, who has hurt herself, "Let me FEEL YOU to see if any bones are broken."

(Remember — daughter ends in "a")

YOU CAN WRITE YOUR ANSWERS IN

○ What is the English for figlia?   _____

○ What is the English for figlio?   _____

○ What is the English for ragazzo?   _____

○ What is the English for ragazza?   _____

○ What is the English for moglie?   _____

○ What is the English for marito?   _____

○ What is the English for sorella?   _____

○ What is the English for fratello?   _____

○ What is the English for madre?   _____

○ What is the English for padre?   _____

TURN BACK FOR THE ANSWERS

COVER UP THE LEFT HAND PAGE BEFORE ANSWERING

○ What is the Italian for daughter? _____

○ What is the Italian for son? _____

○ What is the Italian for boy? _____

○ What is the Italian for girl? _____

○ What is the Italian for wife? _____

○ What is the Italian for husband? _____

○ What is the Italian for sister? _____

○ What is the Italian for brother? _____

○ What is the Italian for mother? _____

○ What is the Italian for father? _____

TURN BACK FOR THE ANSWERS

SOME MORE USEFUL WORDS

THINK OF EACH IMAGE IN YOUR MIND'S EYE FOR ABOUT TEN SECONDS

○ The Italian for YES is SI'   (SEE)
   Imagine you SEE the answer must be YES.

○ The Italian for NO is NO   (NO)
   Imagine shouting "Please, NO spaghetti!"

○ The Italian for NOT is NON   (NON)
   Imagine thinking "I am NOT a NON-person."

○ The Italian for VERY is MOLTO   (MOLTO)
   Imagine MOLTEN lead is VERY hot.

○ The Italian for ONLY is SOLO   (SOLO)
   Imagine thinking "I am the ONLY one going — I am going SOLO."

69

YOU CAN WRITE YOUR ANSWERS IN

○ What is the English for solo?   _____

○ What is the English for molto?   _____

○ What is the English for non?   _____

○ What is the English for no?   _____

○ What is the English for sì?   _____

(Note: When a word is not in capitals, an accent in Italian is always written above the letter.)

TURN BACK FOR THE ANSWERS

COVER UP THE LEFT HAND PAGE BEFORE ANSWERING

○ What is the Italian for only?   _____

○ What is the Italian for very?   _____

○ What is the Italian for not?   _____

○ What is the Italian for no?   _____

○ What is the Italian for yes?   _____

TURN BACK FOR THE ANSWERS

ELEMENTARY GRAMMAR

In this section you will be shown how to use the words AND, BUT and OR.

The Italian for AND is E (The E sounds like "A" in HAY)

Imagine HAY AND straw.

For example,

THE DOG AND THE CAT is IL CANE E IL GATTO

(Remember, the Italian for IS (E') sounds like the "E" in HEN)

The Italian for BUT is MA.

Imagine saying "BUT MA, he's making eyes at me!"

For example,

EXPENSIVE BUT BAD is CARO MA CATTIVO

The Italian for OR is O.

"O" is the first letter of the word OR — it is as if the Italians have forgotten to put the "r" on the word.

For example,

RED OR BLACK is ROSSO O NERO

Now cover up the answers below and translate the following:

(You can write your answers in)

1. THE FATHER WANTS THE BLACK DOG, BUT THE MOTHER WANTS THE WHITE CAT
2. YES, THE SON IS VERY HEAVY AND VERY CLEAN
3. NO, THE WIFE IS NOT UGLY
4. ONLY THE HAT IS VERY DIRTY
5. THE BOY HAS THE RED SHIRT AND THE GIRL HAS THE GREEN DRESS

The answers are:

1. IL PADRE VUOLE IL CANE NERO, MA LA MADRE VUOLE IL GATTO BIANCO
2. SI', IL FIGLIO E' MOLTO PESANTE E MOLTO PULITO
3. NO, LA MOGLIE NON E' BRUTTA
4. SOLO IL CAPPELLO E' MOLTO SPORCO
5. IL RAGAZZO HA LA CAMICIA ROSSA E LA RAGAZZA HA IL VESTITO VERDE

Now cover up the answers below and translate the following:

(You can write your answers in)

1. LA RAGAZZA E' SPORCA, O IL RAGAZZO E' PULITO
2. NO, SOLO LA SCARPA E' PESANTE
3. IL BOTTONE E' MOLTO BRUTTO, E IL VESTITO E' MOLTO PICCOLO
4. LA GIACCA SPORCA E' VERDE E MARRONE, MA NON BIANCA
5. IL CAVALLO HA LA SCARPA ROSSA, E IL GATTO VUOLE LA BLUSA CARA

The answers are:

1. THE GIRL IS DIRTY, OR THE BOY IS CLEAN
2. NO, ONLY THE SHOE IS HEAVY
3. THE BUTTON IS VERY UGLY AND THE DRESS IS VERY SMALL
4. THE DIRTY JACKET IS GREEN AND BROWN, BUT NOT WHITE
5. THE HORSE HAS THE RED SHOE, AND THE CAT WANTS THE EXPENSIVE BLOUSE

ELEMENTARY GRAMMAR

The Italian for A as in A PIG or AN ANIMAL is UN (which sounds like OON).

For example,

A PIG   is UN PORCO

AN ANIMAL is UN ANIMALE

Where the word is feminine, as in A COW or A TABLE, then the word for A is:

UNA

In other words, you add the feminine ending A to UN.

For example,

A COW   is UNA MUCCA

A TABLE is UNA TAVOLA

(Where a feminine word starts with a vowel — for example, APE for BEE — then the word for A is UN', which sounds like the masculine form of A . . . . UN)

Now cover up the answers below and translate the following:

(You can write your answers in)

1. A RED CHAIR IS VERY DIRTY
2. THE BROTHER EATS AN EXPENSIVE CHICKEN
3. THE SISTER WANTS A CLEAN SKIRT
4. THE YELLOW JELLYFISH HAS A RED FISH
5. A BLUE BLOUSE IS VERY DIRTY

The answers are:

1. UNA SEDIA ROSSA E' MOLTO SPORCA
2. IL FRATELLO MANGIA UN POLLO CARO
3. LA SORELLA VUOLE UNA GONNA PULITA
4. LA MEDUSA GIALLA HA UN PESCE ROSSO
5. UNA BLUSA BLU E' MOLTO SPORCA

Now cover up the answers below and translate the following:

(You can write your answers in)

1. IL MARITO HA UN CAVALLO MOLTO CATTIVO, MA LA MOGLIE HA UN'APE PICCOLA

2. SI', LA SORELLA VUOLE UNA CAMICIA ROSSA

3. IL FIGLIO VEDE UNA BLUSA VERDE, MA LA FIGLIA VEDE UNA GIACCA MOLTO NERA

4. SOLO IL BOTTONE E' CARO

5. NO, L'ELASTICO NON E' DURO

The answers are:

1. THE HUSBAND HAS A VERY BAD HORSE, BUT THE WIFE HAS A SMALL BEE

2. YES, THE SISTER WANTS A RED SHIRT

3. THE SON SEES A GREEN BLOUSE, BUT THE DAUGHTER SEES A VERY BLACK JACKET

4. ONLY THE BUTTON IS EXPENSIVE

5. NO, THE ELASTIC IS NOT HARD

Section 4 IN THE COUNTRY/TIME WORDS

**THINK OF EACH IMAGE IN YOUR MIND'S EYE FOR
ABOUT TEN SECONDS**

○ The Italian for GARDEN is GIARDINO   (JARDEENO)
Imagine your elbow being JARRED IN the
garden.

○ The Italian for FLOWER is FIORE   (FYORAY)
Imagine your wife's FURY when you forget
to buy flowers for your anniversary.

○ The Italian for TREE is ALBERO   (ALBERO)
Imagine someone saying "I'LL BARE ALL
if you cut this tree down."

○ The Italian for PLANT is PIANTA   (PYANTA)
Imagine wrapping a plant in a pair of PANTS.

○ The Italian for GRASS is ERBA   (AIRBA)
Imagine using HERBS and grass.

○ The Italian for PATH is SENTIERO   (SENTYAIRO)
Imagine a path running through the
CENTRE of your garden.

○ The Italian for FRUIT is FRUTTA   (FROOTTA)
Imagine FRUIT all covered with spaghetti.

YOU CAN WRITE YOUR ANSWERS IN

○ What is the English for frutta?   _____

○ What is the English for sentiero?   _____

○ What is the English for erba?   _____

○ What is the English for pianta?   _____

○ What is the English for albero?   _____

○ What is the English for fiore?   _____

○ What is the English for giardino?   _____

TURN BACK FOR THE ANSWERS

○ What is the Italian for fruit? _____

○ What is the Italian for path? _____

○ What is the Italian for grass? _____

○ What is the Italian for plant? _____

○ What is the Italian for tree? _____

○ What is the Italian for flower? _____

○ What is the Italian for garden? _____

TURN BACK FOR THE ANSWERS

TIME

THINK OF EACH IMAGE IN YOUR MIND'S EYE FOR ABOUT TEN SECONDS

○ The Italian for TIME is TEMPO   (TEMPO)
Imagine keeping time to the TEMPO of
the music.

○ The Italian for SECOND is SECONDO   (SEKONDO)
Imagine a piece of spaghetti swinging like
a pendulum every SECOND.

○ The Italian for MINUTE is MINUTO   (MEENOOTO)
Imagine trying to eat a plate full of spaghetti
in under a MINUTE.

○ The Italian for HOUR is ORA   (ORA)
Imagine waiting in HORROR for the hour
to strike.

○ The Italian for WEEK is SETTIMANA   (SETTEEMANA)
Imagine a SETTEE MAN visits you once
a week to repair the settee.

○ The Italian for MONTH is MESE   (MAYZAY)
Imagine being lost in a MAZE for a
month.

○ The Italian for YEAR is ANNO   (ANNO)
Imagine an ANNUAL event takes place
once a year.

○ The Italian for DAY is GIORNO   (JORNO)
Imagine a long JOURNEY which takes
you all day.

○ The Italian for NIGHT is (LA) NOTTE   (NOTTAY)
Imagine being NAUGHTY all night.

○ The Italian for TOMORROW is DOMANI   (DOMANEE)
Imagine agreeing to play someone at
DOMINOES tomorrow.

YOU CAN WRITE YOUR ANSWERS IN

○ What is the English for domani? _____

○ What is the English for (la) notte? _____

○ What is the English for giorno? _____

○ What is the English for anno? _____

○ What is the English for mese? _____

○ What is the English for settimana? _____

○ What is the English for ora? _____

○ What is the English for minuto? _____

○ What is the English for secondo? _____

○ What is the English for tempo? _____

TURN BACK FOR THE ANSWERS

COVER UP THE LEFT HAND PAGE BEFORE ANSWERING

○ What is the Italian for tomorrow? _____

○ What is the Italian for night? _____

○ What is the Italian for day? _____

○ What is the Italian for year? _____

○ What is the Italian for month? _____

○ What is the Italian for week? _____

○ What is the Italian for hour? _____

○ What is the Italian for minute? _____

○ What is the Italian for second? _____

○ What is the Italian for time? _____

TURN BACK FOR THE ANSWERS

SOME MORE USEFUL WORDS

THINK OF EACH IMAGE IN YOUR MIND'S EYE FOR ABOUT TEN SECONDS

○ The Italian for MORE is PIU'   (PYOO)
  Imagine there being MORE people than a
  church PEW can hold.

○ The Italian for SOON is PRESTO   (PRESTO)
  Imagine thinking "Hey PRESTO! I'LL SOON
  be rich!"

○ The Italian for ALWAYS is SEMPRE   (SEMPRAY)
  Imagine someone who ALWAYS SIMPERS.

○ The Italian for LESS is MENO   (MAYNO)
  Imagine you have never seen a MENU with
  LESS on it.

○ The Italian for NOW is ADESSO   (ADESSO)
  Imagine someone demanding your ADDRESS
  NOW.

○ The Italian for EVERY is OGNI   (ONYEE)
  Imagine ONIONS with EVERY meal in your
  hotels.

YOU CAN WRITE YOUR ANSWERS IN

○ What is the English for ogni? _____

○ What is the English for adesso? _____

○ What is the English for meno? _____

○ What is the English for sempre? _____

○ What is the English for presto? _____

○ What is the English for più? _____

TURN BACK FOR THE ANSWERS

○ What is the Italian for every? _____

○ What is the Italian for now? _____

○ What is the Italian for less? _____

○ What is the Italian for always? _____

○ What is the Italian for soon? _____

○ What is the Italian for more? _____

TURN BACK FOR THE ANSWERS

Now cover up the answers below and translate the following:

(You can write your answers in)

1. THE DOG EATS THE GRASS NOW

2. THE FATHER WANTS LESS WHITE FISH

3. THE MOTHER EATS MORE FRUIT

4. THE PLANT IS ALWAYS CLEAN, BUT THE TREE IS ALWAYS DIRTY

5. THE DAUGHTER WANTS A GARDEN SOON OR A FLOWER

The answers are:

1. IL CANE MANGIA L'ERBA ADESSO

2. IL PADRE VUOLE MENO PESCE BIANCO

3. LA MADRE MANGIA PIU' FRUTTA

4. LA PIANTA E' SEMPRE PULITA, MA L'ALBERO E' SEMPRE SPORCO

5. LA FIGLIA VUOLE UN GIARDINO PRESTO O UN FIORE

Now cover up the answers below and translate the following:

(You can write your answers in)

1. LA PIANTA E' SEMPRE NERA
2. LA MUCCA VUOLE PIU' FRUTTA E MENO ERBA
3. LA TROTA MANGIA LA MOSCA ADESSO
4. PRESTO LA NOTTE E' GIORNO
5. IL TOPO VEDE UN SENTIERO ADESSO

The answers are:

1. THE PLANT IS ALWAYS BLACK
2. THE COW WANTS MORE FRUIT AND LESS GRASS
3. THE TROUT EATS THE FLY NOW
4. SOON THE NIGHT IS DAY
5. THE RAT SEES A PATH NOW

DAYS OF THE WEEK

THINK OF EACH IMAGE IN YOUR MIND'S EYE FOR ABOUT TEN SECONDS

○ The Italian for MONDAY is LUNEDI'   (LOONAYDEE)
  Imagine Monday being a LOONY DAY.

○ The Italian for TUESDAY is   (MARTAYDEE)
  MARTEDI'
  Imagine MARTYRS being burned on
  Tuesdays.

○ The Italian for WEDNESDAY is   (MAIRKOLAYDEE)
  MERCOLEDI'
  Imagine a MIRACLE LADY passes
  your door every Wednesday.

○ The Italian for THURSDAY is   (JOVAYDEE)
  GIOVEDI'
  Imagine Thursday being a JOVIAL
  DAY.

○ The Italian for FRIDAY is VENERDI'   (VENAIRDEE)
  Imagine putting a VENEER on some
  wood every Friday when you come
  home from work.

○ The Italian for SATURDAY is   (SABATO)
  SABATO
  Imagine Saturday being the Jewish
  SABBATH.

○ The Italian for SUNDAY is   (DOMAYNEEKA)
  DOMENICA
  Imagine DOMINICAN monks praying
  on Sunday.

YOU CAN WRITE YOUR ANSWERS IN

○ What is the English for domenica? _____

○ What is the English for sabato? _____

○ What is the English for venerdì? _____

○ What is the English for giovedì? _____

○ What is the English for mercoledì? _____

○ What is the English for martedì? _____

○ What is the English for lunedì? _____

TURN BACK FOR THE ANSWERS

COVER UP THE LEFT HAND PAGE BEFORE ANSWERING

○ What is the Italian for Sunday?   _____

○ What is the Italian for Saturday?   _____

○ What is the Italian for Friday?   _____

○ What is the Italian for Thursday?   _____

○ What is the Italian for Wednesday?   _____

○ What is the Italian for Tuesday?   _____

○ What is the Italian for Monday?   _____

TURN BACK FOR THE ANSWERS

ELEMENTARY GRAMMAR

The way to ask questions in Italian when you are speaking is by TONE OF VOICE.

You do not change the word order.

For example,

   E' UN TORO? is IS IT A BULL?

In Italian, there is no need for the word IT, I, HE etc., when using a verb.

So,

IT IS A BULL	is E' UN TORO
HE WANTS A BULL	is VUOLE UN TORO
DOES HE WANT A BULL?	is VUOLE UN TORO?

Remember, a question is asked by tone of voice — not by changing the word order.

Now cover up the answers below and translate the following:

(You can write your answers in)

1. IT IS A FLOWER
2. IS IT AN HOUR OR IS IT A DAY?
3. IS HE AN UGLY BOY?
4. SHE IS AN UGLY GIRL
5. HAS SHE A GREEN GARDEN AND A BROWN PATH?

The answers are:

1. E' UN FIORE
2. E' UN'ORA O E' UN GIORNO?
3. E' UN RAGAZZO BRUTTO?
4. E' UNA RAGAZZA BRUTTA
5. HA UN GIARDINO VERDE E UN SENTIERO MARRONE?

Now cover up the answers below and translate the following:

(You can write your answers in)

1. E' LUNEDI' O MARTEDI' DOMANI?
2. E' UN MESE CATTIVO E UN ANNO CATTIVO?
3. E' UN SECONDO RAPIDO MA UN MINUTO LENTO
4. OGNI SETTIMANA HA UN MERCOLEDI', UN GIOVEDI', UN VENERDI', UN SABATO E UNA DOMENICA
5. E' LA NOTTE ADESSO

The answers are:

1. IS IT MONDAY OR TUESDAY TOMORROW?
2. IS IT A BAD MONTH AND A BAD YEAR?
3. IT IS A QUICK SECOND BUT A SLOW MINUTE
4. EVERY WEEK HAS A WEDNESDAY, A THURSDAY, A FRIDAY, A SATURDAY AND A SUNDAY
5. IT IS THE NIGHT NOW

Section 5 IN THE RESTAURANT, NUMBERS, TELLING THE TIME, FOOD AND DRINK

IN THE RESTAURANT

THINK OF EACH IMAGE IN YOUR MIND'S EYE FOR ABOUT TEN SECONDS

○ The Italian for RESTAURANT is (REESTORANTAY)
RISTORANTE
Imagine a RESTAURANT which sells
spaghetti with everything.

○ The Italian for WAITER is (KAMAIRYAIRAY)
CAMERIERE
Imagine a waiter with a CAMERA slung
round his neck.
(Don't confuse with CAMERA — bedroom)

○ The Italian for BILL is CONTO (KONTO)
Imagine COUNTING your bill.

○ The Italian for CUP is TAZZA (TATSA)
Imagine a TASSLE dangling from the
handle of your cup.

○ The Italian for PLATE is PIATTO (PYATTO)
Imagine someone telling you "BE AT
HOME, throw plates around."

○ The Italian for KNIFE is COLTELLO (KOLTELLO)
Imagine wrapping a knife in a COLD TOWEL.

○ The Italian for FORK is FORCHETTA (FORKETTA)
Imagine telling a child not to FORGET A
fork, when he is eating.

○ The Italian for SPOON is CUCCHIAIO (KOOKYA YO)
Imagine a Chinaman with a sheep's eye on
a spoon saying "Now I COOKY-EYE OH!
on a spoon."

○ The Italian for MENU is MENU' (MENOO)
Imagine a MENU which has spaghetti
with everything.

○ The Italian for GLASS is BICCHIERE (BEEKYAIRAY)
Imagine being given a baby's BEAKER
instead of a glass when you ask for a glass.

YOU CAN WRITE YOUR ANSWERS IN

○ What is the English for bicchiere? _____

○ What is the English for menù? _____

○ What is the English for cucchiaio? _____

○ What is the English for forchetta? _____

○ What is the English for coltello? _____

○ What is the English for piatto? _____

○ What is the English for tazza? _____

○ What is the English for conto? _____

○ What is the English for cameriere? _____

○ What is the English for ristorante? _____

TURN BACK FOR THE ANSWERS

○ What is the Italian for glass? _____

○ What is the Italian for menu? _____

○ What is the Italian for spoon? _____

○ What is the Italian for fork? _____

○ What is the Italian for knife? _____

○ What is the Italian for plate? _____

○ What is the Italian for cup? _____

○ What is the Italian for bill? _____

○ What is the Italian for waiter? _____

○ What is the Italian for restaurant? _____

TURN BACK FOR THE ANSWERS

NUMBERS

THINK OF EACH IMAGE IN YOUR MIND'S EYE FOR ABOUT TEN SECONDS

○ The Italian for ONE is UNO   (OONO)
  Imagine YOU KNOW ONE when you see it.

○ The Italian for TWO is DUE   (DOOAY)
  Imagine a DUO, TWO people, singing.

○ The Italian for THREE is TRE   (TRAY)
  Imagine THREE TRAYS.

○ The Italian for FOUR is QUATTRO   (KWATTRO)
  Imagine FOUR QUARTERS.

○ The Italian for FIVE is CINQUE   (CHEENKWAY)
  Imagine the CHINK of FIVE coins.

○ The Italian for SIX is SEI   (SAY)
  Imagine you SAY SIX, six times in Italian:
  say, say, say, say, say, say.

○ The Italian for SEVEN is SETTE   (SETTAY)
  Imagine you have SEVEN SETTEES, one
  for each day of the week.

○ The Italian for EIGHT is OTTO   (OTTO)
  Imagine OTTO the octopus, with EIGHT legs.

○ The Italian for NINE is NOVE   (NOVAY)
  Imagine a German shouting "NEIN! There
  is NO VAY England will score nine goals
  against Germany."

○ The Italian for ZERO is ZERO   (DZAYRO)
  Imagine there is no spaghetti, the stocks are
  ZERO.

YOU CAN WRITE YOUR ANSWERS IN

○ What is the English for zero?   _____

○ What is the English for nove?   _____

○ What is the English for otto?   _____

○ What is the English for sette?   _____

○ What is the English for sei?   _____

○ What is the English for cinque?   _____

○ What is the English for quattro?   _____

○ What is the English for tre?   _____

○ What is the English for due?   _____

○ What is the English for uno?   _____

TURN BACK FOR THE ANSWERS

○ What is the Italian for zero?   _____

○ What is the Italian for nine?   _____

○ What is the Italian for eight?   _____

○ What is the Italian for seven?   _____

○ What is the Italian for six?   _____

○ What is the Italian for five?   _____

○ What is the Italian for four?   _____

○ What is the Italian for three?   _____

○ What is the Italian for two?   _____

○ What is the Italian for one?   _____

TURN BACK FOR THE ANSWERS

ELEMENTARY GRAMMAR

While plurals in Italian are usually very simple, it is best to treat the plurals for masculine and feminine nouns separately.

MASCULINE PLURALS

All masculine nouns, almost without exception, end in "i" (pronounced EE) in the plural.

For example,

    TOPO (rat)   becomes TOPI (rats)

    FIORE (flower) becomes FIORI (flowers)

The word for THE becomes I (pronounced EE) in the plural.

For example,

    IL TORO (the bull)   becomes I TORI (The bulls)

    IL CAMERIERE (the waiter) becomes I CAMERIERI (the waiters)

You will remember that where a word starts with a vowel, for example ALBERO, the word for THE is L'.

So,

    THE TREE is L'ALBERO

    THE BIRD is L'UCCELLO

For these words, the word for THE becomes GLI (pronounced like LEE) in the plural. For example,

    L'UCCELLO (the bird) becomes GLI UCCELLI (the birds)

    L'ALBERO (the tree)   becomes GLI ALBERI (the trees)

Now cover up the answers below and translate the following:

(You can write your answers in)

1. THE BOY HAS TWO BROTHERS
2. THE BEAR EATS THE CHICKENS EVERY DAY
3. THE HUSBAND WANTS FOUR KNIVES, THREE PLATES AND SIX GLASSES
4. THE SON SEES THE BIRDS
5. THE WIFE WANTS NINE FLOWERS

The answers are:

1. IL RAGAZZO HA DUE FRATELLI
2. L'ORSO MANGIA I POLLI OGNI GIORNO
3. IL MARITO VUOLE QUATTRO COLTELLI, TRE PIATTI E SEI BICCHIERI
4. IL FIGLIO VEDE GLI UCCELLI
5. LA MOGLIE VUOLE NOVE FIORI

Now cover up the answers below and translate the following:

(You can write your answers in)

1. IL RAGAZZO HA OTTO CONTI E LA RAGAZZA VUOLE DUE CONTI

2. IL FIGLIO VEDE I DUE COLTELLI

3. IL CAMERIERE VUOLE QUATTRO PIATTI, TRE FORCHETTE E I CINQUE BICCHIERI

4. LA SORELLA VEDE GLI ASINI, E LA MADRE VEDE GLI ALBERI, MA IL FRATELLO NON VEDE GLI ORSI

5. IL BRUCO HA I NOVE GIARDINI

The answers are:

1. THE BOY HAS EIGHT BILLS AND THE GIRL WANTS TWO BILLS

2. THE SON SEES THE TWO KNIVES

3. THE WAITER WANTS FOUR PLATES, THREE FORKS AND THE FIVE GLASSES

4. THE SISTER SEES THE DONKEYS, AND THE MOTHER SEES THE TREES, BUT THE BROTHER DOES NOT SEE THE BEARS

5. THE CATERPILLAR HAS THE NINE GARDENS

ELEMENTARY GRAMMAR

FEMININE PLURALS
Again, feminine plurals are straightforward.
All feminine nouns ending in "a" change to "e".

For example,

FORCHETTA (fork) becomes FORCHETTE (forks)

SORELLA (sister)   becomes SORELLE (sisters)

The word for THE in the plural is always LE, whether the word starts with a vowel or not.

For example,

LA RANA (the frog) becomes LE RANE (the frogs)

L'ORA (the hour)   becomes LE ORE (the hours)

The rules that you have been given cover the great majority of words.

Occasionally you will make mistake.

Now cover up the answers below and translate the following:

(You can write your answers in)

1. THE DUCK EATS SIX FROGS
2. THE GIRL HAS EIGHT HOURS
3. THE SISTER WANTS THE TABLES AND THE CHAIRS
4. THE CAT HAS TWO SHOES AND FIVE CUPS
5. THE MOTHER WANTS FOUR PLATES AND SEVEN SKIRTS

The answers are:

1. L'ANITRA MANGIA SEI RANE
2. LA RAGAZZA HA OTTO ORE
3. LA SORELLA VUOLE LE TAVOLE E LE SEDIE
4. IL GATTO HA DUE SCARPE E CINQUE TAZZE
5. LA MADRE VUOLE QUATTRO PIATTI E SETTE GONNE

Now cover up the answers below and translate the following:

(You can write your answers in)

1. IL CAMERIERE VUOLE LE DUE PIANTE

2. IL MARITO HA LE QUATTRO TENDE, LE CINQUE PORTE E LE OTTO SEDIE, MA NON LE TRE FINESTRE O LE DUE TAVOLE

3. IL GATTO VEDE LE ERBE, I CASSETTI E LE FINESTRE

4. LA RANA VEDE LA FRUTTA

5. VEDE IL CAVALLO E LE SCALE

The answers are:

1. THE WAITER WANTS THE TWO PLANTS

2. THE HUSBAND HAS THE FOUR CURTAINS, THE FIVE DOORS AND THE EIGHT CHAIRS, BUT NOT THE THREE WINDOWS OR THE TWO TABLES

3. THE CAT SEES THE GRASSES, THE DRAWERS AND THE WINDOWS

4. THE FROG SEES THE FRUIT

5. HE SEES THE HORSE AND THE STAIRS

FOOD AND DRINK

THINK OF EACH IMAGE IN YOUR MIND'S EYE FOR ABOUT TEN SECONDS

○ The Italian for BREAD is PANE   (PANAY)
Imagine a PAN full of bread.

○ The Italian for BUTTER is BURRO   (BOORRO)
Imagine a writing BUREAU smeared with butter.

○ The Italian for WINE is VINO   (VEENO)
Imagine a German saying "VE KNOW what the best wine is."

○ The Italian for WATER is ACQUA   (AKWA)
Imagine an AQUADUCT bringing water to your hotel.

○ The Italian for MILK is LATTE   (LATTAY)
Imagine a LATIN teacher drinking milk whilst reciting Latin verbs.

○ The Italian for SALT is SALE   (SALAY)
Imagine sprinkling salt on your SALAD.

○ The Italian for PEPPER is PEPE   (PAYPAY)
Imagine someone demanding PAY! PAY! for the pepper you have used.

○ The Italian for COFFEE is CAFFE'   (KAFFE)
Imagine drinking coffee in a CAFE.

○ The Italian for TEA is TE'   (TE)
Imagine pouring TEA all over your spaghetti.

○ The Italian for JAM is MARMELLATA   (MARMELLATA)
Imagine mixing jam and MARMALADE on your bread.

YOU CAN WRITE YOUR ANSWERS IN

○ What is the English for marmellata? _____

○ What is the English for tè? _____

○ What is the English for caffè? _____

○ What is the English for pepe? _____

○ What is the English for sale? _____

○ What is the English for latte? _____

○ What is the English for acqua? _____

○ What is the English for vino? _____

○ What is the English for burro? _____

○ What is the English for pane? _____

TURN BACK FOR THE ANSWERS

COVER UP THE LEFT HAND PAGE BEFORE ANSWERING

○ What is the Italian for jam?   _____

○ What is the Italian for tea?   _____

○ What is the Italian for coffee?   _____

○ What is the Italian for pepper?   _____

○ What is the Italian for salt?   _____

○ What is the Italian for milk?   _____

○ What is the Italian for water?   _____

○ What is the Italian for wine?   _____

○ What is the Italian for butter?   _____

○ What is the Italian for bread?   _____

TURN BACK FOR THE ANSWERS

ELEMENTARY GRAMMAR

Adjectives also become plural in Italian, and they change their endings to agree with the word they go with.

(This is exactly the same kind of thing that is done in the singular, where an adjective has to agree with the noun.)

For example,

BLACK DOGS   is CANI NERI

BLACK FROGS is RANE NERE

Where an adjective already ends in an "e", for example VERDE (green), then it changes to end in an "i" (VERDI) no matter what the gender of the noun.

So,

    GREEN DOGS   is CANI VERDI

    GREEN FROGS   is RANE VERDI

Finally, the word for ARE is SONO.

Imagine asking if you ARE the SON O' your father.

    To say: THE DOGS ARE HEAVY   you say I CANI SONO PESANTI

    To say: THE TABLES ARE UGLY you say LE TAVOLE SONO BRUTTE

Where one word is masculine and the other feminine, for example:

    THE DOG AND THE FROG ARE BLACK

then the adjective takes the MASCULINE form:

    IL CANE E LA RANA SONO NERI

Now cover up the answers below and translate the following:

(You can write your answers in)

1. THE RESTAURANTS ARE EMPTY
2. THE GLASSES ARE FULL
3. THE CHAIRS ARE HIGH
4. THE BEDS ARE VERY CLEAN
5. ARE THE WAITERS QUICK?

The answers are:

1. I RISTORANTI SONO VUOTI
2. I BICCHIERI SONO PIENI
3. LE SEDIE SONO ALTE
4. I LETTI SONO MOLTO PULITI
5. I CAMERIERI SONO RAPIDI?

Now cover up the answers below and translate the following:

(You can write your answers in)

1. ADESSO L'ACQUA, LE TAZZE STRETTE E I PIATTI PROFONDI SONO VERDI

2. IL MENU' E' CARO OGNI GIORNO MA IL PANE E IL LATTE SONO FRESCHI

   (FRESCHI is pronounced FRESKEE)

3. IL CAFFE' E IL TE' SONO PULITI, MA IL PEPE E LA MARMELLATA SONO SPORCHI

   (SPORCHI is pronounced SPORKEE)

4. IL VINO E LA FORCHETTA SONO PESANTI

5. MANGIA IL BURRO E IL PANE DURO

The answers are:

1. NOW THE WATER, THE NARROW CUPS AND THE DEEP PLATES ARE GREEN

2. THE MENU IS EXPENSIVE EVERY DAY BUT THE BREAD AND THE MILK ARE FRESH

3. THE COFFEE AND THE TEA ARE CLEAN, BUT THE PEPPER AND THE JAM ARE DIRTY

4. THE WINE AND THE FORK ARE HEAVY

5. HE (or SHE or IT) EATS THE BUTTER AND THE HARD BREAD

TELLING THE TIME (1)

THINK OF EACH IMAGE IN YOUR MIND'S EYE FOR ABOUT TEN SECONDS

The next part of Section 5 deals with telling the time. However, first you will need to know some more numbers and words.

○ The Italian for TEN is DIECI   (DYAYCHEE)
   Imagine a DIET SHEET with
   TEN colours for everything.

○ The Italian for ELEVEN is UNDICI   (OONDEECHEE)
   Imagine punching ELEVEN
   footballers ON THE CHIN.

○ The Italian for MIDDAY is   (MEDZOJORNO)
   MEZZOGIORNO
   Imagine an Italian MADE THE
   JOURNEY at MIDDAY.

○ The Italian for MIDNIGHT is   (MEDZANOTTAY)
   MEZZANOTTE
   Imagine an Italian waiter MADE
   ZE NAUGHTY suggestion at
   MIDNIGHT.

○ The Italian for QUARTER is QUARTO   (KWARTO)
   Imagine cutting your spaghetti
   into QUARTERS.

○ The Italian for HALF is MEZZO   (MEDZO)
   Imagine the MED'S SO dirty
   HALF the population will not
   swim in it. (A mezzo soprano is
   half a soprano.)

○ The Italian for TWENTY is VENTI   (VENTEE)
   Imagine a German whose
   eyesight is VENTI-VENTI.

○ The Italian for TWENTY-FIVE is (VENTEECHEENKWAY)
   VENTICINQUE
   Imagine you add twenty and five
   together. (VENTI and CINQUE)

YOU CAN WRITE YOUR ANSWERS IN

○ What is the English for venticinque?   _____

○ What is the English for venti?   _____

○ What is the English for mezzo?   _____

○ What is the English for quarto?   _____

○ What is the English for mezzogiorno?   _____

○ What is the English for mezzanotte?   _____

○ What is the English for undici?   _____

○ What is the English for dieci?   _____

TURN BACK FOR THE ANSWERS

○ What is the Italian for 25? _____

○ What is the Italian for 20? _____

○ What is the Italian for half? _____

○ What is the Italian for quarter? _____

○ What is the Italian for midnight? _____

○ What is the Italian for midday? _____

○ What is the Italian for eleven? _____

○ What is the Italian for ten? _____

TURN BACK FOR THE ANSWERS

TELLING THE TIME (2)

As you learned earlier the Italian for THE HOUR is L'ORA, which is of course feminine. The Italian for WHAT is CHE (pronounced KAY).

The Italian for WHAT TIME IS IT? is CHE ORA E' (What hour is?).

To answer this question in Italian with, for example, IT'S ONE O'CLOCK, TWO O'CLOCK etc., the literal translation is IT IS THE ONE, THEY ARE THE TWO, THEY ARE THE THREE, etc.

The word for HOUR is not said but is understood.

So,

IT IS ONE O'CLOCK is IT IS THE ONE (E' L'UNA)

IT IS TWO O'CLOCK is THEY ARE THE TWO (SONO LE DUE)

Note that the word for THE is feminine because the word for HOUR is feminine.

IT IS THREE O'CLOCK   is THEY ARE THE THREE (SONO LE TRE)

IT IS ELEVEN O'CLOCK is THEY ARE THE ELEVEN (SONO LE UNDICI)

Now cover up the answers below and translate the following:

(You can write your answers in)

1. IT IS FIVE O'CLOCK
2. IT IS THREE O'CLOCK
3. IT IS SEVEN O'CLOCK
4. IT IS FOUR O'CLOCK
5. IT IS ONE O'CLOCK

The answers are:

1. SONO LE CINQUE
2. SONO LE TRE
3. SONO LE SETTE
4. SONO LE QUATTRO
5. E' L'UNA

TELLING THE TIME (3)

To say it is MIDNIGHT or MIDDAY you simply say:

E' MEZZANOTTE   (It is midnight)

E' MEZZOGIORNO (It is midday)

so you miss out the word THE.

When you want to say IT IS FIVE PAST SEVEN or TEN PAST EIGHT, etc., then you say THEY ARE SEVEN AND FIVE, etc.

So,

IT IS FIVE PAST THREE   is THEY ARE THE THREE
AND FIVE
(SONO LE TRE E CINQUE)

IT IS TEN PAST TEN   is THEY ARE THE TEN
AND TEN
(SONO LE DIECI E DIECI)

IT IS HALF PAST SIX   is THEY ARE THE SIX
AND HALF
(SONO LE SEI E MEZZO)

For IT IS A QUARTER PAST SIX, however, you say
THEY ARE THE SIX
AND A QUARTER
(SONO LE SEI E UN QUARTO)

Now cover up the answers below and translate the following:

(You can write your answers in)

1. IT IS TEN PAST FOUR
2. IT IS FIVE PAST NINE
3. IT IS HALF PAST THREE
4. IT IS QUARTER PAST EIGHT
5. IT IS QUARTER PAST SIX

The answers are:

1. SONO LE QUATTRO E DIECI
2. SONO LE NOVE E CINQUE
3. SONO LE TRE E MEZZO
4. SONO LE OTTO E UN QUARTO
5. SONO LE SEI E UN QUARTO

TELLING THE TIME (4)

When you want to say IT IS TEN TO FOUR or TWENTY TO FOUR, then in Italian you say THEY ARE FOUR MINUS TWENTY.

In Italian this is SONO LE QUATTRO MENO VENTI.

So,

IT IS FIVE TO THREE   is THEY ARE THE THREE
MINUS FIVE
(SONO LE TRE MENO CINQUE)

A QUARTER TO EIGHT is THEY ARE THE EIGHT
MINUS A QUARTER
(SONO LE OTTO MENO UN
QUARTO)

Remember, if it is QUARTER to ONE, then you say E' L'UNA MENO UN QUARTO.

Now cover up the answers below and translate the following:

(You can write your answers in)

1. IT IS QUARTER TO FOUR
2. IT IS QUARTER PAST TWELVE (midnight)
3. IT IS TWENTY-FIVE TO THREE
4. IT IS TWENTY PAST TWELVE (midday)
5. IT IS TEN TO SEVEN
6. IT IS FIVE TO ELEVEN
7. IT IS HALF PAST THREE
8. IT IS HALF PAST ONE

The answers are:

1. SONO LE QUATTRO MENO UN QUARTO
2. E' MEZZANOTTE E UN QUARTO
3. SONO LE TRE MENO VENTICINQUE
4. E' MEZZOGIORNO E VENTI
5. SONO LE SETTE MENO DIECI
6. SONO LE UNDICI MENO CINQUE
7. SONO LE TRE E MEZZO
8. E' L'UNA E MEZZO

PLEASE NOTE: To say AT 2 O'CLOCK you simply say ALLE DUE.

AT HALF PAST SIX is ALLE SEI E MEZZO

AT MIDDAY   is A MEZZOGIORNO etc.

(A and ALLE will be dealt with more fully later on.)

Section 6 MORE FOOD AND DRINK

THINK OF EACH IMAGE IN YOUR MIND'S EYE FOR ABOUT TEN SECONDS

○ The Italian for SOUP is MINESTRA   (MEENESTRA)
Imagine MINESTRONE soup.

○ The Italian for MEAT is (LA) CARNE   (KARNAY)
Imagine CARNIVORES eating meat.

○ The Italian for LAMB is AGNELLO   (ANYELLO)
Imagine AN all-YELLOW lamb.

○ The Italian for STEAK is BISTECCA   (BEESTEKKA)
Imagine asking for a BEEFSTEAK and
spaghetti.

○ The Italian for PEA is PISELLO   (PEEZELLO)
Imagine meeting a tin of peas for the first
time and saying "PEAS HELLO".

○ The Italian for GARLIC is AGLIO   (ALYO)
Imagine thinking that ALL YOU need to
put someone off is to eat garlic.

○ The Italian for CARROT is CAROTA   (KAROTA)
Imagine spaghetti and CARROTS.

○ The Italian for CABBAGE is CAVOLO   (KAVOLO)
Imagine throwing cabbage at a charging
CAVALRY.

○ The Italian for ONION is CIPOLLA   (CHEEPOLLA)
Imagine CHIPOLLATA sausages and
pickled onions.

○ The Italian for MUSHROOM is FUNGO   (FOONGO)
Imagine that the FUNGI that you collect are
all edible mushrooms.

YOU CAN WRITE YOUR ANSWERS IN

○ What is the English for fungo? _____

○ What is the English for cipolla? _____

○ What is the English for cavolo? _____

○ What is the English for carota? _____

○ What is the English for aglio? _____

○ What is the English for pisello? _____

○ What is the English for bistecca? _____

○ What is the English for agnello? _____

○ What is the English for carne? _____

○ What is the English for minestra? _____

TURN BACK FOR THE ANSWERS

COVER UP THE LEFT HAND PAGE BEFORE ANSWERING

○ What is the Italian for mushroom? _____

○ What is the Italian for onion? _____

○ What is the Italian for cabbage? _____

○ What is the Italian for carrot? _____

○ What is the Italian for garlic? _____

○ What is the Italian for pea? _____

○ What is the Italian for steak? _____

○ What is the Italian for lamb? _____

○ What is the Italian for meat? _____

○ What is the Italian for soup? _____

TURN BACK FOR THE ANSWERS

THINK OF EACH IMAGE IN YOUR MIND'S EYE FOR ABOUT TEN SECONDS

○ The Italian for EGGS is UOVA (WOVA)
Imagine you WOVE A cloth with pictures of eggs on it.

○ The Italian for OMELETTE is FRITTATA (FREETTATA)
Imagine telling someone "If this omelette is FREE — TA! TA! I'm off. It can't be any good."

○ The Italian for TOMATO is POMODORO (POMODORO)
Imagine a sea COMMODORE eating tomatoes on the deck on his ship.

○ The Italian for POTATO is PATATA (PATATA)
Imagine eating spaghetti and mashed POTATOES.

○ The Italian for VEAL is VITELLO (VEETELLO)
Imagine a German waiter saying "VE TELL YOU to eat veal in this restaurant."

○ The Italian for CAKE is TORTA (TORTA)
Imagine all the cakes in Italy are TARTS.

○ The Italian for APPLE is MELA (MAYLA)
Imagine someone who MAILS YOU apples.

○ The Italian for PEAR is PERA (PAYRA)
Imagine a PAIR A pears.

○ The Italian for MELON is MELONE (MAYLONAY)
Imagine MELON stuffed with spaghetti.

○ The Italian for LEMONADE is LIMONATA (LEEMONATA)
Imagine pouring a bottle of LEMONADE over your spaghetti.

YOU CAN WRITE YOUR ANSWERS IN

○ What is the English for limonata? _____

○ What is the English for melone? _____

○ What is the English for pera? _____

○ What is the English for mela? _____

○ What is the English for torta? _____

○ What is the English for vitello? _____

○ What is the English for patata? _____

○ What is the English for pomodoro? _____

○ What is the English for frittata? _____

○ What is the English for uova? _____

TURN BACK FOR THE ANSWERS

○ What is the Italian for lemonade?   _____

○ What is the Italian for melon?   _____

○ What is the Italian for pear?   _____

○ What is the Italian for apple?   _____

○ What is the Italian for cake?   _____

○ What is the Italian for veal?   _____

○ What is the Italian for potato?   _____

○ What is the Italian for tomato?   _____

○ What is the Italian for omelette?   _____

○ What is the Italian for eggs?   _____

TURN BACK FOR THE ANSWERS

ELEMENTARY GRAMMAR

As we learned in the last section, the word for ARE is SONO.

The word for

   (THEY) EAT   is MANGIANO
   (THEY) WANT is VOGLIONO
   (THEY) HAVE is HANNO
   (THEY) SEE   is VEDONO

Notice that they all end in "NO".

So, THEY EAT THE VEAL is MANGIANO IL VITELLO

To say THE DOGS EAT THE VEAL
you say I CANI MANGIANO IL VITELLO

   THE SONS WANT THE MOTHER is I FIGLI VOGLIONO
                                       LA MADRE
   THE CATS HAVE THE CARROTS is I GATTI HANNO LE
                                       CAROTE
   THE GIRLS SEE THE WAITER   is LE RAGAZZE
                                       VEDONO IL
                                       CAMERIERE

REMEMBER THAT

   HAS (e.g. he has)   is HA
   WANTS (e.g he wants) is VUOLE
   EATS (e.g. he eats)   is MANGIA
   SEES (e.g. he sees)   is VEDE

However:

   I HAVE is HO   I EAT is MANGIO
   I WANT is VOGLIO   I SEE is VEDO

They all end in "O".

So,

   I EAT A COW   is MANGIO UNA MUCCA
   I SEE A LAMB is VEDO UN AGNELLO

Note that you do not normally say "I" in Italian.

The word HO means I HAVE, the word VEDO means I SEE, etc.

Similarly, HA means HE, SHE or IT HAS, etc.

Now cover up the answers below and translate the following:

(You can write your answers in)

1. THE BLACK RATS EAT THE YELLOW APPLES AND THE RED CARROTS
2. THE HUSBAND AND THE WIFE HAVE TWO DAUGHTERS
3. I SEE THE WATER
4. THE BEDS AND THE DRAWERS ARE EMPTY
5. THE BROTHERS WANT MORE WINE

The answers are:

1. I TOPI NERI MANGIANO LE MELE GIALLE E LE CAROTE ROSSE
2. IL MARITO E LA MOGLIE HANNO DUE FIGLIE
3. VEDO L'ACQUA
4. I LETTI E I CASSETTI SONO VUOTI
5. I FRATELLI VOGLIONO PIU' VINO

Now cover up the answers below and translate the following:

(You can write your answers in)

1. IL MARITO E LA MOGLIE MANGIANO DUE AGNELLI NERI E L'AGLIO

2. DUE FRITTATE SONO SEMPRE PICCOLE, MA LA MINESTRA NON E' CARA

3. PRESTO LE CAROTE E LE PATATE SONO NERE

4. LA SORELLA E IL FRATELLO VOGLIONO SETTE TORTE ADESSO

5. I LETTI SONO PICCOLI

The answers are:

1. THE HUSBAND AND THE WIFE EAT TWO BLACK LAMBS AND THE GARLIC

2. TWO OMELETTES ARE ALWAYS SMALL, BUT THE SOUP IS NOT EXPENSIVE

3. SOON THE CARROTS AND THE POTATOES ARE BLACK

4. THE SISTER AND THE BROTHER WANT SEVEN CAKES NOW

5. THE BEDS ARE SMALL

SOME MORE USEFUL WORDS

THINK OF EACH IMAGE IN YOUR MIND'S EYE FOR ABOUT TEN SECONDS

○ The Italian for ON is SU   (SOO)
Imagine someone SUES you ON the slightest pretext.

○ The Italian for IN is IN   (EEN)
Imagine being covered IN spaghetti.

○ The Italian for AT and TO is A   (A)
Imagine saying "AH, I know what he's AT, but I don't know what TO do."

○ The Italian for OF is DI   (DEE)
Imagine the D of DUNDEE.

○ The Italian for FROM is DA   (DA)
Imagine a baby getting a cuddle FROM DA DA.

YOU CAN WRITE YOUR ANSWERS IN

○ What is the English for DA? _____

○ What is the English for DI? _____

○ What is the English for A? _____

○ What is the English for IN? _____

○ What is the English for SU? _____

TURN BACK FOR THE ANSWERS

○ What is the Italian for from? _____

○ What is the Italian for of? _____

○ What is the Italian for at or to? _____

○ What is the Italian for in? _____

○ What is the Italian for on? _____

TURN BACK FOR THE ANSWERS

Now cover up the answers below and translate the following:

(You can write your answers in)

1. THE DOG IS ON A CHAIR, BUT THE CAT IS ON A TABLE
2. THE BUTTER IS IN A CUPBOARD, AND THE BREAD IS IN A DRAWER
3. THE SOUP AND THE MEAT ARE FROM A RESTAURANT
4. THE HUSBAND SEES THE WIFE AT A RESTAURANT
5. THE SISTER WANTS A PLATE OF PEAS AND A GLASS OF WHITE WINE

The answers are:

1. IL CANE E' SU UNA SEDIA, MA IL GATTO E' SU UNA TAVOLA
2. IL BURRO E' IN UN ARMADIO, E IL PANE E' IN UN CASSETTO
3. LA MINESTRA E LA CARNE SONO DA UN RISTORANTE
4. IL MARITO VEDE LA MÓGLIE A UN RISTORANTE
5. LA SORELLA VUOLE UN PIATTO DI PISELLI E UN BICCHIERE DI VINO BIANCO

Now cover up the answers below and translate the following:

(You can write your answers in)

1. LA BISTECCA E' SU UNA TAVOLA GIALLA

2. LE ANITRE MANGIANO LE UOVA DURE IN UNA STANZA

3. HO UN PIATTO DI CIPOLLE E UN PIATTO DI POMODORI

4. IL CAMERIERE HA UN FUNGO DA UN RISTORANTE E UN CAVOLO DA UN GIARDINO

5. LE PERE E LA LIMONATA SONO SU UNA SEDIA O SU UN TAPPETO, MA IL MELONE E IL VITELLO SONO IN UN CASSETTO

The answers are:

1. THE STEAK IS ON A YELLOW TABLE

2. THE DUCKS EAT THE HARD EGGS IN A ROOM

3. I HAVE A PLATE OF ONIONS AND A PLATE OF TOMATOES

4. THE WAITER HAS A MUSHROOM FROM A RESTAU-RANT AND A CABBAGE FROM A GARDEN

5. THE PEARS AND THE LEMONADE ARE ON A CHAIR OR ON A CARPET, BUT THE MELON AND THE VEAL ARE IN A DRAWER

Section 7   SHOPPING AND BUSINESS WORDS

THINK OF EACH IMAGE IN YOUR MIND'S EYE FOR ABOUT TEN SECONDS

○ The Italian for OWNER is   (PROPREE AYTAREEO)
  PROPRIETARIO
  Imagine asking to see the
  PROPRIETOR, the owner of the business.

○ The Italian for MANAGER is   (DEERETTORAY)
  DIRETTORE
  Imagine asking to see the
  manager, and the managing
  DIRECTOR is brought to see you.

○ The Italian for BOSS is PADRONE   (PADRONAY)
  Imagine the boss of a firm,
  PATRONISED by everyone.

○ The Italian for WORK is LAVORO   (LAVORO)
  Imagine being told to LOVE OR
  work, but not both.

○ The Italian for FACTORY is FABBRICA   (FABBREEKA)
  Imagine a factory making FABRICS.

○ The Italian for SALARY or   (SALAREEO)
  WAGE is SALARIO
  Imagine spending your SALARY
  on spaghetti.

○ The Italian for PRODUCT is PRODOTTO   (PRODOTTO)
  Imagine a factory whose sole
  PRODUCT is spaghetti.

○ The Italian for FIRM is DITTA   (DEETTA)
  Imagine making a DETOUR to
  look over a firm.

○ The Italian for CHEQUE is ASSEGNO   (ASSENYO)
  Imagine I SEND YOU a cheque.

○ The Italian for OFFICE is UFFICIO   (OOFEECHO)
  Imagine telling a girl in your office
  "YOUR FEET SHOW."

YOU CAN WRITE YOUR ANSWERS IN

○ What is the English for ufficio? _____

○ What is the English for assegno? _____

○ What is the English for ditta? _____

○ What is the English for prodotto? _____

○ What is the English for salario? _____

○ What is the English for fabbrica? _____

○ What is the English for lavoro? _____

○ What is the English for padrone? _____

○ What is the English for direttore? _____

○ What is the English for proprietario? _____

TURN BACK FOR THE ANSWERS

COVER UP THE LEFT HAND PAGE BEFORE ANSWERING

○ What is the Italian for office?   _____

○ What is the Italian for cheque?   _____

○ What is the Italian for firm?   _____

○ What is the Italian for product?   _____

○ What is the Italian for salary/wage?   _____

○ What is the Italian for factory?   _____

○ What is the Italian for work?   _____

○ What is the Italian for boss?   _____

○ What is the Italian for manager?   _____

○ What is the Italian for owner?   _____

TURN BACK FOR THE ANSWERS

ELEMENTARY GRAMMAR

As we saw in the last section, there is no problem about any prepositions with the word "a".

For example,

ON A CAT is SU UN GATTO.

However, when you use the word THE, for example ON THE CAT, then things get a bit more complicated.

What you do is to join the word for ON to the word for THE.

For example,

Join SU and IL so that ON THE becomes SUL.

Therefore, ON THE CAT becomes SUL GATTO (NOT su il gatto).

Similarly AT THE becomes AL, so that AT THE DRAWER becomes AL CASSETTO (NOT a il cassetto) and so on.

For feminine nouns, you also run the words ON and THE (la) together:

ON THE TABLE	becomes	SULLA TAVOLA
AT THE TABLE	is	ALLA TAVOLA
FROM THE TABLE	is	DALLA TAVOLA

Now cover up the answers below and translate the following:

(You can write your answers in)

1. THE DOG EATS FROM THE FLOOR
2. THE MANAGER IS ON THE CARPET
3. THE BOSS IS AT THE FACTORY
4. THE PRODUCT IS AT THE DOOR
5. THE CHEQUE IS FROM THE MOTHER

The answers are:

1. IL CANE MANGIA DAL PAVIMENTO
2. IL DIRETTORE E' SUL TAPPETO
3. IL PADRONE E' ALLA FABBRICA
4. IL PRODOTTO E' ALLA PORTA
5. L'ASSEGNO E' DALLA MADRE

Now cover up the answers below and translate the following:

(You can write your answers in)

1. IL PROPRIETARIO E' SULLA TAVOLA
2. IL SALARIO E' MOLTO PICCOLO
3. IL PROPRIETARIO E IL DIRETTORE SONO AL RISTORANTE
4. GLI ASSEGNI SONO SEMPRE SPORCHI
5. IL RAGAZZO E' ALLA DITTA

The answers are:

1. THE OWNER IS ON THE TABLE
2. THE SALARY IS VERY SMALL
3. THE OWNER AND THE MANAGER ARE AT THE RESTAURANT
4. THE CHEQUES ARE ALWAYS DIRTY
5. THE BOY IS AT THE FIRM

MORE BUSINESS WORDS

THINK OF EACH IMAGE IN YOUR MIND'S EYE FOR ABOUT TEN SECONDS

○ The Italian for GOODS is (LA) MERCE   (MAIRCHAY)
  Imagine goods and MERCHANDISE.

○ The Italian for HOLIDAYS is VACANZE   (VAKANTSAY)
  Imagine there is a VACANCY because of holidays.

○ The Italian for PRICE is PREZZO   (PRETSO)
  Imagine asking the price of a PRETZEL.

○ The Italian for MISTAKE is ERRORE   (ERRORAY)
  Imagine your work being full of mistakes
  and ERRORS.

○ The Italian for MARKET is MERCATO   (MAIRKATO)
  Imagine a MARKET where all they sell
  is spaghetti.

○ The Italian for SHOP is NEGOZIO   (NAYGOTSEEO)
  Imagine NEGOTIATING the price of
  goods in a shop.

○ The Italian for SHOP ASSISTANT is   (KOMMESSA)
  COMMESSA
  Imagine a shop assistant saying
  "COME HERE, SIR and try this on."

○ The Italian for CASH DESK is CASSA   (KASSA)
  Imagine handing over your CASH AT a
  cash desk.

○ The Italian for SECRETARY is   (SEGRETAREEA)
  SEGRETARIA
  Imagine your SECRETARY all covered
  in spaghetti.

○ The Italian for WORKER is OPERAIO   (OPER Y O)**
  Imagine an OPERATIVE worker in a factory.

** Note: in this pronunciation, the Y is as in the English "my"

153

YOU CAN WRITE YOUR ANSWERS IN

○ What is the English for operaio? _____

○ What is the English for segretaria? _____

○ What is the English for cassa? _____

○ What is the English for commessa? _____

○ What is the English for negozio? _____

○ What is the English for mercato? _____

○ What is the English for errore? _____

○ What is the English for prezzo? _____

○ What is the English for vacanze? _____

○ What is the English for merce? _____

TURN BACK FOR THE ANSWERS

○ What is the Italian for worker?   _____

○ What is the Italian for secretary?   _____

○ What is the Italian for cash desk?   _____

○ What is the Italian for shop assistant?   _____

○ What is the Italian for shop?   _____

○ What is the Italian for market?   _____

○ What is the Italian for mistake?   _____

○ What is the Italian for price?   _____

○ What is the Italian for holidays?   _____

○ What is the Italian for goods?   _____

TURN BACK FOR THE ANSWERS

ELEMENTARY GRAMMAR

Words like IN and OF also change when they are used with the word THE.

IN and THE

You will remember that IN A DRAWER is IN UN CASSETTO

However,

IN THE DRAWER becomes NEL CASSETTO
(Imagine Little NELL dead IN THE drawer)

For feminine nouns, NEL becomes NELLA.

So,

IN THE ROOM becomes NELLA STANZA

OF and THE

Similarly the word OF becomes DEL when used with THE.

So,

OF THE DOG becomes DEL CANE

(Imagine thinking OF THE DELL)

For feminine nouns DEL becomes DELLA

So,
OF THE ONION becomes DELLA CIPOLLA

Now cover up the answers below and translate the following:

(You can write your answers in)

1. THE CASH DESK IS IN THE SHOP
2. THE SECRETARY OF THE FIRM IS IN THE ROOM
3. THE PRICE OF THE HAT IS HIGH
4. THE CHEQUE IS IN THE JACKET
5. THE WORKER IS IN THE FACTORY

The answers are:

1. LA CASSA E' NEL NEGOZIO
2. LA SEGRETARIA DELLA DITTA E' NELLA STANZA
3. IL PREZZO DEL CAPPELLO E' ALTO
4. L'ASSEGNO E' NELLA GIACCA
5. L'OPERAIO E' NELLA FABBRICA

Now cover up the answers below and translate the following:

(You can write your answer in)

1. L'UFFICIO DELLA DITTA E' NELLA FABBRICA
2. HA UN NEGOZIO NEL MERCATO
3. IL PREZZO DI UN OPERAIO E' MOLTO CARO
4. LA COMMESSA E' ALLA FABBRICA
5. LE MERCI SONO IN UN ARMADIO

The answers are:

1. THE OFFICE OF THE FIRM IS IN THE FACTORY
2. HE (or SHE) HAS A SHOP IN THE MARKET
3. THE PRICE OF A WORKER IS VERY EXPENSIVE
4. THE SHOP ASSISTANT IS AT THE FACTORY
5. THE GOODS ARE IN A CUPBOARD

Section 8 TRAVELLING, THE CAR

THINK OF EACH IMAGE IN YOUR MIND'S EYE FOR ABOUT TEN SECONDS

○ The Italian for PASSPORT is PASSAPORTO (PASSAPORTO)
Imagine spilling spaghetti all over your PASSPORT.

○ The Italian for CUSTOMS is DOGANA (DOGANA)
Imagine declaring a DOG AND A cat to customs.

○ The Italian for MONEY EXCHANGE is CAMBIO (KAMBYO)
Imagine you CAN BUY money at the money exchange.

○ The Italian for MONEY is DANARO (DANARO)
Imagine buying DINNER with your money.

○ The Italian for TICKET is BIGLIETTO (BEELYETTO)
Imagine someone asking if you have had the BILL YET for your tickets.

○ The Italian for TOILET is GABINETTO (GABEENETTO)
Imagine a kitchen CABINET being used as a toilet.

○ The Italian for ENTRANCE is ENTRATA (ENTRATA)
Imagine ENTRANCE TO your hotel all covered with spaghetti.

○ The Italian for EXIT is USCITA (OOSHEETA)
Imagine someone shouting "YOU CHEATER" as you run for the exit.

○ The Italian for STATION is (LA) STAZIONE (STATSYONAY)
Imagine a STATION platform all covered in spaghetti.

○ The Italian for DANGER is PERICOLO (PAYREEKOLO)
Imagine the famous singer PERRY COMO shouting to you — Danger! Danger!

YOU CAN WRITE YOUR ANSWERS IN

○ What is the English for pericolo?   _____

○ What is the English for stazione?   _____

○ What is the English for uscita?   _____

○ What is the English for entrata?   _____

○ What is the English for gabinetto?   _____

○ What is the English for biglietto?   _____

○ What is the English for danaro?   _____

○ What is the English for cambio?   _____

○ What is the English for dogana?   _____

○ What is the English for passaporto?   _____

TURN BACK FOR THE ANSWERS

COVER UP THE LEFT HAND PAGE BEFORE ANSWERING

○ What is the Italian for danger? _____

○ What is the Italian for station? _____

○ What is the Italian for exit? _____

○ What is the Italian for entrance? _____

○ What is the Italian for toilet? _____

○ What is the Italian for ticket? _____

○ What is the Italian for money? _____

○ What is the Italian for money exchange? _____

○ What is the Italian for customs? _____

○ What is the Italian for passport? _____

TURN BACK FOR THE ANSWERS

ELEMENTARY GRAMMAR

The Italian for AM, for example I AM A FATHER, is SONO.

So,

I AM A FATHER is SONO UN PADRE

Please note that the word "I" is normally missed out in Italian. In fact all personal pronouns like I, he, she, it, etc., are nearly always missed out (but you need not worry about the exceptions).

So,

SHE IS A MOTHER is E' UNA MADRE

IT IS A TICKET is E' UN BIGLIETTO

REMEMBER that when you say something like I AM TIRED the sentence in Italian is either SONO STANCO or SONO STANCA depending on whether the speaker is male or female.

Also, when you say something like IT IS DIRTY, then the gender of whatever IT refers to will affect the ending of the adjective.

For example, if "it" is a table then

IT IS DIRTY is E' SPORCA (Because TAVOLA is feminine)

If "it" is a dog then

IT IS DIRTY is E' SPORCO
(because CANE is masculine)

Now cover up the answers below and translate the following:

(You can write your answers in)

1. I AM ALWAYS TIRED
2. IT IS A DIRTY PASSPORT
3. HE HAS MONEY AND A TICKET
4. SHE WANTS THE TOILET
5. IT IS THE EXIT FROM THE STATION

The answers are:

1. SONO SEMPRE STANCO (or STANCA)
2. E' UN PASSAPORTO SPORCO
3. HA DANARO E UN BIGLIETTO
4. VUOLE IL GABINETTO (You can also use the word TOILETTE — pronounced TWALET.)
5. E' L'USCITA DALLA STAZIONE

SOME MORE TRAVEL WORDS

THINK OF EACH IMAGE IN YOUR MIND'S EYE FOR ABOUT TEN SECONDS

○ The Italian for BOAT is BATTELLO   (BATTELLO)
   Imagine sailing into BATTLE on a boat.

○ The Italian for TRAIN is TRENO   (TRAYNO)
   Imagine a TRAIN with spaghetti trailing
   from every window.

○ The Italian for CAR is MACCHINA   (MAKKEENA)
   Imagine your car as a shiny new MACHINE.

○ The Italian for STREET is STRADA   (STRADA)
   Imagine a group of people STRADDLING
   the street.

○ The Italian for BRIDGE is PONTE   (PONTAY)
   Imagine a group of people all POINT TO a bridge.

○ The Italian for MAP is MAPPA   (MAPPA)
   Imagine a MAP all covered in little bits of
   spaghetti.

○ The Italian for PETROL is BENZINA   (BENTSEENA)
   Imagine a sign at a petrol station
   "BENZINE for sale".

○ The Italian for OIL is OLIO   (OLYO)
   Imagine someone threatening to OIL YOU
   by pouring a can of oil over your head.

○ The Italian for GARAGE is GARAGE   (GARAJ)
   Imagine a GARAGE forecourt all covered in
   spaghetti.

○ The Italian for TRAFFIC LIGHTS is   (SAYMAFORO)
   SEMAFORO
   Imagine traffic lights have broken down and
   a policeman is using SEMAPHORE flags
   instead to direct traffic.

YOU CAN WRITE YOUR ANSWERS IN

○ What is the English for semaforo?   _____

○ What is the English for garage?   _____

○ What is the English for olio?   _____

○ What is the English for benzina?   _____

○ What is the English for mappa?   _____

○ What is the English for ponte?   _____

○ What is the English for strada?   _____

○ What is the English for macchina?   _____

○ What is the English for treno?   _____

○ What is the English for battello?   _____

TURN BACK FOR THE ANSWERS

COVER UP THE LEFT HAND PAGE BEFORE ANSWERING

○ What is the Italian for traffic lights? _____

○ What is the Italian for garage? _____

○ What is the Italian for oil? _____

○ What is the Italian for petrol? _____

○ What is the Italian for map? _____

○ What is the Italian for bridge? _____

○ What is the Italian for street? _____

○ What is the Italian for car? _____

○ What is the Italian for train? _____

○ What is the Italian for boat? _____

TURN BACK FOR YOUR ANSWERS

SOME MORE USEFUL WORDS

THINK OF EACH IMAGE IN YOUR MIND'S EYE FOR ABOUT TEN SECONDS

○ The Italian for HERE is QUI   (KWEE)
  Imagine being told that the QUEEn is HERE.

○ The Italian for THERE is LI'   (LEE)
  Imagine thinking "THERE in yonder LEE, I
  would like to be."

○ The Italian for FIRST is PRIMO   (PREEMO)
  Imagine having a PREMONITION that you
  will be FIRST in your class.

○ The Italian for LAST is ULTIMO   (OOLTEEMO)
  Imagine giving an ULTIMATUM — a LAST
  warning.

○ The Italian for SECOND is SECONDO   (SAYKONDO)
  Imagine asking for a SECOND helping of
  spaghetti.

YOU CAN WRITE YOUR ANSWERS IN

○ What is the English for secondo? _____

○ What is the English for ultimo? _____

○ What is the English for primo? _____

○ What is the English for lì? _____

○ What is the English for qui? _____

TURN BACK FOR THE ANSWERS

COVER UP THE LEFT HAND PAGE BEFORE ANSWERING

○ What is the Italian for second? _____

○ What is the Italian for last? _____

○ What is the Italian for first? _____

○ What is the Italian for there? _____

○ What is the Italian for here? _____

TURN BACK FOR THE ANSWERS

ELEMENTARY GRAMMAR

Whilst almost all adjectives come after the noun:

For example,

   GATTO NERO   for BLACK CAT

   MARITO BRUTTO for UGLY HUSBAND

the words PRIMO, ULTIMO and SECONDO come before the noun.

So,

   IT IS THE FIRST BOAT is E' IL PRIMO BATTELLO

   IT IS THE LAST TRAIN is E' L'ULTIMO TRENO

Now cover up the answers below and translate the following:

(You can write your answers in)

1. THE FIRST BOAT IS HERE
2. THE LAST TRAIN IS IN THE STATION
3. THE STREET IS HERE
4. THE SECOND BRIDGE IS THERE
5. THE ENTRANCE IS THERE

The answers are:

1. IL PRIMO BATTELLO E' QUI
2. L'ULTIMO TRENO E' NELLA STAZIONE
3. LA STRADA E' QUI
4. IL SECONDO PONTE E' LI'
5. L'ENTRATA E' LI'

Now cover up the answers below and translate the following:

(You can write your answers in)

1. LA MACCHINA E' PESANTE E NERA
2. IL CAMBIO E' LI', MA E' CARO
3. PERICOLO! LA DOGANA E' QUI
4. I SEMAFORI SONO SEMPRE ROSSI QUI
5. IL GARAGE HA LA MAPPA E L'OLIO

The answers are:

1. THE CAR IS HEAVY AND BLACK
2. THE MONEY EXCHANGE IS THERE, BUT IT IS EXPENSIVE
3. DANGER! THE CUSTOMS IS HERE
4. THE TRAFFIC LIGHTS ARE ALWAYS RED HERE
5. THE GARAGE HAS THE MAP AND THE OIL

MORE TRAVELLING WORDS

THINK OF EACH IMAGE IN YOUR MIND'S EYE FOR ABOUT TEN SECONDS

○ The Italian for BREAKDOWN is GUASTO   (GWASTO)
Imagine telling the garage that something
GHASTLY has happened, you have broken down.

○ The Italian for DRIVER is AUTISTA   (OWTEESTA)
Imagine an ARTIST driving a car, with an
easel and paint in the back.

○ The Italian for BRAKE is FRENO   (FRAYNO)
Imagine being told "Don't be AFRAID,
the brakes do work."

○ The Italian for SPARKING PLUG is   (KANDAYLA)
CANDELA
Imagine using CANDLES instead of
sparking plugs, in your car.

○ The Italian for BONNET is COFANO   (KOFANO)
Imagine a COFFIN being placed on the
bonnet of your car.

○ The Italian for BATTERY is BATTERIA   (BATTAIREEA)
Imagine a BATTERY covered in spaghetti.

○ The Italian for WHEEL is RUOTA   (RWOTA)
Imagine a wheel on the end of your ROTOR blades.

○ The Italian for TYRE is GOMMA   (GOMMA)
Imagine your tyre made of GUMMY
material and going all soft.

○ The Italian for STEERING WHEEL is   (VOLANTAY)
VOLANTE
Imagine VIOLENTLY grabbing at the
steering wheel.

○ The Italian for JACK is CRICCO   (KREEKO)
Imagine being up the CREEK without a
jack after a puncture.

YOU CAN WRITE YOUR ANSWERS IN

○ What is the English for cricco?   _____

○ What is the English for volante?   _____

○ What is the English for gomma?   _____

○ What is the English for ruota?   _____

○ What is the English for batteria?   _____

○ What is the English for cofano?   _____

○ What is the English for candela?   _____

○ What is the English for freno?   _____

○ What is the English for autista?   _____

○ What is the English for guasto?   _____

TURN BACK FOR THE ANSWERS

COVER UP THE LEFT HAND PAGE BEFORE ANSWERING

○ What is the Italian for jack?   _____

○ What is the Italian for steering wheel?   _____

○ What is the Italian for tyre?   _____

○ What is the Italian for wheel?   _____

○ What is the Italian for battery?   _____

○ What is the Italian for bonnet?   _____

○ What is the Italian for sparking plug?   _____

○ What is the Italian for brake?   _____

○ What is the Italian for driver?   _____

○ What is the Italian for breakdown?   _____

TURN BACK FOR THE ANSWERS

SOME MORE USEFUL WORDS

THINK OF EACH IMAGE IN YOUR MIND'S EYE FOR ABOUT TEN SECONDS

○ The Italian for WHERE is DOVE   (DOVAY)
  Imagine asking "WHERE is DOVER?"

○ The Italian for WHY is PERCHE'   (PAIRKAY)
  Imagine asking "WHY are you so PERKY?"

○ The Italian for WHICH is QUALE   (KWALAY)
  Imagine asking "WHICH KOALA bear do you
  want?"

○ The Italian for HOW MUCH is QUANTO   (KWANTO)
  Imagine asking "HOW MUCH is the bottle of
  COINTREAU?"

○ The Italian for WHO is CHI   (KEE)
  Imagine wondering WHO has got your KEY.

YOU CAN WRITE YOUR ANSWERS IN

○ What is the English for chi? _____

○ What is the English for quanto? _____

○ What is the English for quale? _____

○ What is the English for perchè? _____

○ What is the English for dove? _____

TURN BACK FOR THE ANSWERS

COVER UP THE LEFT HAND PAGE BEFORE ANSWERING

○ What is the Italian for who? _____

○ What is the Italian for how much? _____

○ What is the Italian for which? _____

○ What is the Italian for why? _____

○ What is the Italian for where? _____

TURN BACK FOR THE ANSWERS

ELEMENTARY GRAMMAR

Please note that when the word DOVE (where) is used with the word IS, for example, WHERE IS THE DOG?, then WHERE IS becomes DOV'E', with the stress on the E'.

So,

WHERE IS THE DOG? is DOV'E' IL CANE?

Now cover up the answers below and translate the following:

(You can write your answers in)

1. WHERE IS THE PASSPORT? — IT IS HERE
2. WHO IS THE GIRL?
3. WHY AM I HERE?
4. HOW MUCH IS THE PETROL?
5. WHICH HORSE IS FIRST?

The answers are:

1. DOV'E' IL PASSAPORTO? — E' QUI
2. CHI E' LA RAGAZZA?
3. PERCHE' SONO QUI?
4. QUANTO E' LA BENZINA?
5. QUALE CAVALLO E' PRIMO?

Now cover up the answers below and translate the following:

(You can write your answers in)

1. LA MACCHINA E PESANTE E NERA, E IL GUASTO E CATTIVO

2. DOV'E' LA BATTERIA, E DOV'E' LA GOMMA?

3. IL FRENO, PERCHE' E' SPORCO, E LA CANDELA, PERCHE' E' VERDE?

4. CHI E' L'AUTISTA, E' DOV'E' IL CRICCO?

5. IL COFANO E LA RUOTA SONO MOLTO DURI, MA IL VOLANTE PERCHE' NON E' PULITO?

The answers are:

1. THE CAR IS HEAVY AND BLACK, AND THE BREAKDOWN IS BAD

2. WHERE IS THE BATTERY, AND WHERE IS THE TYRE?

3. WHY IS THE BRAKE DIRTY AND WHY IS THE SPARKING PLUG GREEN?

4. WHO IS THE DRIVER AND WHERE IS THE JACK?

5. THE BONNET AND THE WHEEL ARE VERY HARD, BUT WHY IS THE STEERING WHEEL NOT CLEAN?

·Notice that in a question involving the word WHY (PERCHE') the subject of the question is often placed first, with PERCHE' and the verb following.

Section 9 LEISURE ACTIVITY

ON THE BEACH

THINK OF EACH IMAGE IN YOUR MIND'S EYE FOR ABOUT TEN SECONDS

○ The Italian for SEA is MARE   (MARAY)
   Imagine you watch a couple MARRY in the sea.

○ The Italian for BAY is BAIA   (BY YA)
   Imagine a rich man boasting "I'll BUY YOU
   this bay."

○ The Italian for SAND is SABBIA   (SABBYA)
   Imagine that sand SAPS YOUR strength
   when you walk on it.

○ The Italian for SUN is SOLE   (SOLAY)
   Imagine the sun shining SO YOU'LAY on the beach.

○ The Italian for HOT is CALDO   (KALDO)
   Imagine COLD water comes out of the hot tap.

○ The Italian for COLD is FREDDO   (FREDDO)
   Imagine being AFRAID O' the cold.

○ The Italian for BUCKET is SECCHIA   (SEKKYA)
   Imagine if you are SICK YOU can use a bucket.

○ The Italian for PICNIC is PICNIC   (PEEKNEEK)
   Imagine you have cold spaghetti for your
   PICNIC.

○ The Italian for HELP is AIUTO   (AYOOTO)
   Imagine shouting "AH! YOU TWO help me!"

○ The Italian for GAME is GIUOCO   (JOKO)
   Imagine the game you are playing is a bit of a JOKE.

YOU CAN WRITE YOUR ANSWERS IN

○ What is the English for giuoco? _____

○ What is the English for aiuto? _____

○ What is the English for picnic? _____

○ What is the English for secchia? _____

○ What is the English for freddo? _____

○ What is the English for caldo? _____

○ What is the English for sole? _____

○ What is the English for sabbia? _____

○ What is the English for baia? _____

○ What is the English for mare? _____

TURN BACK FOR THE ANSWERS

COVER UP THE LEFT HAND PAGE BEFORE ANSWERING

○ What is the Italian for game? _____

○ What is the Italian for help? _____

○ What is the Italian for picnic? _____

○ What is the Italian for bucket? _____

○ What is the Italian for cold? _____

○ What is the Italian for hot? _____

○ What is the Italian for sun? _____

○ What is the Italian for sand? _____

○ What is the Italian for bay? _____

○ What is the Italian for sea? _____

TURN BACK FOR THE ANSWERS

MORE LEISURE WORDS

THINK OF EACH IMAGE IN YOUR MIND'S EYE FOR ABOUT TEN SECONDS

○ The Italian for COUNTRYSIDE is CAMPAGNA (KAMPANYA)
Imagine going with a COMPANION into the countryside.

○ The Italian for RIVER is FIUME (FYOOMAY)
Imagine a river going so fast that FEW MAY get across.

○ The Italian for MOUNTAIN is MONTAGNA (MONTANYA)
Imagine the American state of MONTANA, with high mountains.

○ The Italian for LAKE is LAGO (LAGO)
Imagine a lake filled with LAGER beer.

○ The Italian for NEWSPAPER is GIORNALE (JORNALAY)
Imagine a JOURNAL made up of old newspapers.

○ The Italian for BOOK is LIBRO (LEEBRO)
Imagine a LIBRARY full of books.

○ The Italian for LETTER is LETTERA (LETTERA)
Imagine a LETTER all covered in spaghetti.

○ The Italian for STAMP is FRANCOBOLLO (FRANKOBOLLO)
Imagine when you want to send a ball by post, they FRANK A BALL OH! with a franking machine instead of putting a stamp on it.

○ The Italian for ENVELOPE is BUSTA (BOOSTA)
Imagine you BUST An envelope open when you are buying a packet of them.

○ The Italian for EXCURSION is GITA (JEETA)
Imagine saying "GEE TA!" when someone offers to take you on an exciting excursion.

189

YOU CAN WRITE YOUR ANSWERS IN

○ What is the English for gita? _____

○ What is the English for busta? _____

○ What is the English for francobollo? _____

○ What is the English for lettera? _____

○ What is the English for libro? _____

○ What is the English for giornale? _____

○ What is the English for lago? _____

○ What is the English for montagna? _____

○ What is the English for fiume? _____

○ What is the English for campagna? _____

TURN BACK FOR THE ANSWERS

COVER UP THE LEFT HAND PAGE BEFORE ANSWERING

○ What is the Italian for excursion?   _____

○ What is the Italian for envelope?   _____

○ What is the Italian for stamp?   _____

○ What is the Italian for letter?   _____

○ What is the Italian for book?   _____

○ What is the Italian for newspaper?   _____

○ What is the Italian for lake?   _____

○ What is the Italian for mountain?   _____

○ What is the Italian for river?   _____

○ What is the Italian for countryside?   _____

TURN BACK FOR THE ANSWERS

ELEMENTARY GRAMMAR

You will remember that the Italian for I AM is SONO.

In Italian the word for:

   I EAT   is MANGIO

   I HAVE is HO

   I WANT is VOGLIO

   I SEE   is VEDO

In other words, all of these verbs end in an "o" when you say I WANT, I SEE, etc.

Please note that you use the same word if you want to say I AM EATING, etc. Remember, "I" always ends in "o".

For example,

   I SEE A DOG   is VEDO UN CANE

   I WANT A PASSPORT   is VOGLIO UN PASSAPORTO

   I AM EATING A DUCK is MANGIO UN'ANITRA

   I HAVE A BUCKET   is HO UNA SECCHIA

Please note, also, that MANGIA for EATS can also be used to say HE IS EATING.

Similarly, VEDE can mean HE or SHE IS SEEING as well as HE or SHE SEES, and so on for all verbs.

Now cover up the answers below and translate the following:

(You can write your answers in)

1. I SEE THE BLUE SEA AND THE GOLDEN SAND
2. I WANT THE GAME HERE, NOT THERE
3. THE SUN IS VERY HOT BUT THE RIVER IS COLD
4. I AM EATING A PICNIC ON THE LAKE
5. I HAVE A NEWSPAPER AND AN EXPENSIVE BOOK

The answers are:

1. VEDO IL MARE BLU E LA SABBIA D'ORO
2. VOGLIO IL GIUOCO QUI, NON LI'
3. IL SOLE E' MOLTO CALDO MA IL FIUME E' FREDDO
4. MANGIO UN PICNIC SUL LAGO
5. HO UN GIORNALE E UN LIBRO CARO

Now cover up the answers below and translate the following:

(You can write your answers in)

1. IL CANE VUOLE LA SECCHIA PESANTE, E VUOLE LE LETTERE ROSSE

2. LA GITA E' MOLTO TRANQUILLA E IL PICNIC E' CATTIVO

3. GIORGIO HA UN LIBRO SPORCO E VEDE UNA BAIA SPORCA

4. AIUTO! VEDO LA MONTAGNA FREDDA E LA CAMPAGNA MARRONE

5. VOGLIO IL SOLE CALDO E VOGLIO IL MARE FREDDO

The answers are:

1. THE DOG WANTS THE HEAVY BUCKET AND HE WANTS THE RED LETTERS

2. THE EXCURSION IS VERY QUIET AND THE PICNIC IS BAD

3. GIORGIO HAS A DIRTY BOOK AND HE SEES A DIRTY BAY

4. HELP! I SEE THE COLD MOUNTAIN AND THE BROWN COUNTRYSIDE

5. I WANT THE HOT SUN AND I WANT THE COLD SEA

SOME MORE USEFUL WORDS

THINK OF EACH IMAGE IN YOUR MIND'S EYE FOR ABOUT TEN SECONDS

○ The Italian for I DRINK is BEVO   (BAYVO)
  Imagine DRINKING a BEVERAGE.

○ The Italian for I PUT is METTO   (METTO)
  Imagine I PUT METAL on a table.

○ The Italian for I SPEAK is PARLO   (PARLO)
  Imagine people SPEAKING in the PARLOUR.

○ The Italian for I SELL is VENDO   (VENDO)
  Imagine a street VENDOR SELLING you
  something.

NOTE that you use the same words for I AM DRINKING, I AM
GOING, etc.

YOU CAN WRITE YOUR ANSWERS IN

○ What is the English for vendo?   _____

○ What is the English for parlo?   _____

○ What is the English for metto?   _____

○ What is the English for bevo?   _____

TURN BACK FOR THE ANSWERS

COVER UP THE LEFT HAND PAGE BEFORE ANSWERING

○ What is the Italian for I sell?   _____

○ What is the Italian for I speak?   _____

○ What is the Italian for I put?   _____

○ What is the Italian for I drink?   _____

TURN BACK FOR THE ANSWERS

GENERALLY USEFUL WORDS

THINK OF EACH IMAGE IN YOUR MIND'S EYE FOR ABOUT TEN SECONDS

○ The Italian for DOCTOR is DOTTORE   (DOTTORAY)
Imagine a DODDERY old doctor
listening to your chest.

○ The Italian for DENTIST is (IL)   (DENTEESTA)
DENTISTA
Imagine a DENTIST with spaghetti
between his teeth.

○ The Italian for LAWYER is AVVOCATO   (AVVOKATO)
Imagine a lawyer eating an AVOCADO pear.

○ The Italian for POLICEMAN is   (POLEETSYOTTO)
POLIZIOTTO
Imagine a policeman standing on a
POLICE YACHT OH!

○ The Italian for BANK is BANCA   (BANKA)
Imagine depositing spaghetti in a BANK.

○ The Italian for HOTEL is ALBERGO   (ALBAIRGO)
Imagine you ALL BARE GO into your hotel.
(Remember the word for TREE is ALBERO).

○ The Italian for HOSPITAL is   (OSPAYDALAY)
OSPEDALE
Imagine they give you nothing but
spaghetti in HOSPITAL.

○ The Italian for CHURCH is CHIESA   (KYAYZA)
Imagine you have the KEYS OF a church.

○ The Italian for MUSEUM is MUSEO   (MOOZAYO)
Imagine an exhibition of spaghetti in a
MUSEUM.

○ The Italian for CASTLE is CASTELLO   (KASTELLO)
Imagine Lou COSTELLO of Abbot and
Costello, looking over the parapet of a castle.

199

YOU CAN WRITE YOUR ANSWERS IN

○ What is the English for castello?   _____

○ What is the English for museo?   _____

○ What is the English for chiesa?   _____

○ What is the English for ospedale?   _____

○ What is the English for albergo?   _____

○ What is the English for banca?   _____

○ What is the English for poliziotto?   _____

○ What is the English for avvocato?   _____

○ What is the English for dentista?   _____

○ What is the English for dottore?   _____

TURN BACK FOR THE ANSWERS

COVER UP THE LEFT HAND PAGE BEFORE ANSWERING

○ What is the Italian for castle? _____

○ What is the Italian for museum? _____

○ What is the Italian for church? _____

○ What is the Italian for hospital? _____

○ What is the Italian for hotel? _____

○ What is the Italian for bank? _____

○ What is the Italian for policeman? _____

○ What is the Italian for lawyer? _____

○ What is the Italian for dentist? _____

○ What is the Italian for doctor? _____

TURN BACK FOR THE ANSWERS

Now cover up the answers below and translate the following:

(You can write your answers in)

1. I AM DRINKING A GLASS OF HOT MILK
2. I AM AT THE CHURCH
3. I AM PUTTING A STAMP ON THE ENVELOPE
4. I AM SPEAKING TO THE DOCTOR, BUT NOT TO THE LAWYER
5. I AM SELLING A HOTEL AND A CASTLE

The answers are:

1. BEVO UN BICCHIERE DI LATTE CALDO
2. SONO ALLA CHIESA
3. METTO UN FRANCOBOLLO SULLA BUSTA
4. PARLO AL DOTTORE, MA NON ALL'AVVOCATO
5. VENDO UN ALBERGO E UN CASTELLO

PLEASE NOTE:

When the noun begins with a vowel, for example AVVOCATO, then AL or ALLA becomes ALL'.

AL and ALL' sound very similar.

Now cover up the answers below and translate the following:

(You can write your answers in)

1. VENDO LA SABBIA CALDA
2. AIUTO! METTO LA LETTERA SULLA TAVOLA
3. VENDO IL FRANCOBOLLO
4. PARLO AL MARITO
5. BEVO IL VINO

The answers are:

1. I AM SELLING THE HOT SAND
2. HELP! I AM PUTTING THE LETTER ON THE TABLE
3. I AM SELLING THE STAMP
4. I AM SPEAKING TO THE HUSBAND
5. I AM DRINKING THE WINE

ELEMENTARY GRAMMAR

You will remember from an earlier section that when you want to say THEY EAT, THEY WANT, etc., then the word ends in NO.

So,

THEY WANT is VOGLIONO

THEY EAT   is MANGIANO

THEY HAVE is HANNO

THEY SEE   is VEDONO

Similarly, the same is true of the words you learned in the last section.

So,

THEY DRINK is BEVONO

THEY PUT   is METTONO

THEY SPEAK is PARLANO

THEY SELL   is VENDONO

For example,

THEY DRINK THE TEA   is BEVONO IL TE'

THEY DRINK IN A ROOM is BEVONO IN UNA STANZA

THEY SPEAK TO A FROG is PARLANO A UNA RANA

NOTE:

If one says:

THE BOY AND THE GIRL SPEAK, SEE, etc., then the words for SPEAK and SEE are PARLANO and VEDONO, etc.

Now cover up the answers below and translate the following:

(You can write your answers in)

1. THE BOY AND THE GIRL DRINK IN THE RESTAURANT
2. THE FISH AND THE HORSE SPEAK TO THE BULL
3. THE BROTHER AND THE SISTER SELL A HEAVY CHAIR
4. THE BUCKET AND THE SAND ARE IN THE ROOM
5. THE HUSBAND AND THE WIFE PUT THE STAMP ON THE ENVELOPE

The answers are:

1. IL RAGAZZO E LA RAGAZZA BEVONO NEL RISTORANTE
2. IL PESCE E IL CAVALLO PARLANO AL TORO
3. IL FRATELLO E LA SORELLA VENDONO UNA SEDIA PESANTE
4. LA SECCHIA E LA SABBIA SONO NELLA STANZA
5. IL MARITO E LA MOGLIE METTONO IL FRANCOBOLLO SULLA BUSTA

Now cover up the answers below and translate the following:

(You can write your answers in)

1. AIUTO! DOV'E' L'OSPEDALE? VOGLIO UN DOTTORE O
   UN DENTISTA
2. IL POLIZIOTTO VEDE LA BANCA
3. PARLO E BEVO
4. IL MUSEO HA QUATTRO STANZE STRETTE
5. BEVO IL VINO, MANGIO IL PANE, VEDO LE RAGAZZE
   CATTIVE E SONO STANCO

The answers are:

1. HELP! WHERE IS THE HOSPITAL? I WANT A DOCTOR
   OR A DENTIST
2. THE POLICEMAN SEES THE BANK
3. I SPEAK AND DRINK
4. THE MUSEUM HAS FOUR NARROW ROOMS
5. I DRINK THE WINE, I EAT THE BREAD, I SEE THE BAD
   GIRLS AND I AM TIRED

ELEMENTARY GRAMMAR

You will remember that:

HE HAS   is HA

HE EATS is MANGIA

HE SEES is VEDE

So, the word either ends in an "a" or an "e".

It is exactly the same for the words you have just learned.

So,

HE DRINKS is BEVE

HE PUTS   is METTE

SHE SELLS is VENDE

HE SPEAKS is PARLA

(He, she and it are the same word.)

So,

HE SELLS THE CUPS   is VENDE LE TAZZE

SHE DRINKS THE WINE   is BEVE IL VINO

SHE SPEAKS TO THE DOG is PARLA AL CANE

Remember that there is no need to say HE, SHE or IT in Italian. The form of the verb is the same in all three cases.

Now cover up the answers below and translate the following:

(You can write your answers in)

1. SHE HAS A FLOWER AND SHE SELLS THE PLANTS
2. HE DRINKS THE WINE AND HE SPEAKS TO THE SON
3. SHE PUTS THE NEWSPAPER ON THE TABLE
4. SHE IS EATING IN A RESTAURANT AND SHE SELLS THE MEAT TO THE RESTAURANT
5. SHE SEES THE LETTERS AND SHE HAS THE BOOKS

The answers are:

1. HA UN FIORE E VENDE LE PIANTE
2. BEVE IL VINO E PARLA AL FIGLIO
3. METTE IL GIORNALE SULLA TAVOLA
4. MANGIA IN UN RISTORANTE E VENDE LA CARNE AL RISTORANTE
5. VEDE LE LETTERE E HA I LIBRI

Now cover up the answers below and translate the following:

(You can write your answers in)

1. METTO UN LIBRO SULLA TAVOLA
2. IL BRUCO E LA MEDUSA BEVONO DAL PIATTO
3. VENDONO COLTELLI, PIATTI E FORCHETTE
4. IL PADRE E LA MADRE VEDONO I MARI
5. IL FIGLIO BEVE, LA FIGLIA MANGIA, IL FRATELLO PARLA E LA MADRE VENDE LA SABBIA

The answers are:

1. I AM PUTTING A BOOK ON THE TABLE
2. THE CATERPILLAR AND THE JELLYFISH DRINK FROM THE PLATE
3. THEY SELL KNIVES, PLATES AND FORKS
4. THE FATHER AND THE MOTHER SEE THE SEAS
5. THE SON DRINKS, THE DAUGHTER EATS, THE BROTHER SPEAKS AND THE MOTHER SELLS THE SAND

Section 10 AT THE DOCTOR'S, EMERGENCY WORDS, USEFUL WORDS

ILLNESS

THINK OF EACH IMAGE IN YOUR MIND'S EYE FOR ABOUT TEN SECONDS

○ The Italian for FOOT is PIEDE   (PYAYDAY)
  Imagine your wife putting her foot down when
  it comes to PAY DAY.

○ The Italian for SICK is MALATO   (MALATO)
  Imagine being sick with a mysterious MALADY.

○ The Italian for HEAD is TESTA   (TESTA)
  Imagine a doctor who TESTS A head to see if it
  is still O.K.

○ The Italian for SKIN is (LA) PELLE   (PELLAY)
  Imagine the famous footballer PELE, with his
  glistening skin.

○ The Italian for HEART is CUORE   (KWORAY)
  Imagine throwing someone's heart into a
  QUARRY.

○ The Italian for BACK is DORSO   (DORSO)
  Imagine the DORSAL fin on the back of a shark.

○ The Italian for THIGH is COSCIA   (KOSHA)
  Imagine one Rabbi asking another Rabbi
  whether a lady's thigh is KOSHER.

○ The Italian for STOMACH is STOMACO (STOMAKO)
  Imagine your STOMACH full up with spaghetti.

○ The Italian for HAND is (LA) MANO   (MANO)
  Imagine a MAN warming his hand.

○ The Italian for LEG is GAMBA   (GAMBA)
  Imagine GAMBOLling about on a gammy leg.

YOU CAN WRITE YOUR ANSWERS IN

○ What is the English for gamba? _____

○ What is the English for (la) mano? _____

○ What is the English for stomaco? _____

○ What is the English for coscia? _____

○ What is the English for dorso? _____

○ What is the English for cuore? _____

○ What is the English for (la) pelle? _____

○ What is the English for testa? _____

○ What is the English for malato? _____

○ What is the English for piede? _____

TURN BACK FOR THE ANSWERS

COVER UP THE LEFT HAND PAGE BEFORE ANSWERING

○ What is the Italian for leg?   _____

○ What is the Italian for hand?   _____

○ What is the Italian for stomach?   _____

○ What is the Italian for thigh?   _____

○ What is the Italian for back?   _____

○ What is the Italian for heart?   _____

○ What is the Italian for skin?   _____

○ What is the Italian for head?   _____

○ What is the Italian for sick?   _____

○ What is the Italian for foot?   _____

TURN BACK FOR THE ANSWERS

EMERGENCY AND USEFUL WORDS

THINK OF EACH IMAGE IN YOUR MIND'S EYE FOR ABOUT TEN SECONDS

- The Italian for BANDAGE is FASCIA   (FASHA)
  Imagine a FASCIST with a bandage
  round his arm.

- The Italian for BLOOD is SANGUE   (SANGWAY)
  Imagine someone who SANG AWAY
  as blood streamed from his head.

- The Italian for ACCIDENT is   (EENCHEEDENTAY)
  INCIDENTE
  Imagine a nasty INCIDENT results
  in an accident.

- The Italian for THIEF is LADRO   (LADRO)
  Imagine a thief with a LADDER ON
  his back, running down a street.

- The Italian for FIRE is FUOCO   (FWOKO)
  Imagine a fire at a garage FORECOURT.

- The Italian for TELEPHONE is   (TELAYFONO)
  TELEFONO
  Imagine a TELEPHONE all covered
  in spaghetti.

- The Italian for AMBULANCE is   (AMBOOLANTSA)
  AMBULANZA
  Imagine loading spaghetti into an
  AMBULANCE.

- The Italian for LOST is PERSO   (PAIRSO)
  Imagine a POOR SOUL who is lost.

- The Italian for DEAD is MORTO   (MORTO)
  Imagine someone showing he is
  MORTAL by being dead.

- The Italian for PAIN is DOLORE   (DOLORAY)
  Imagine being given a DOLLAR to
  make your pain go away.

YOU CAN WRITE YOUR ANSWERS IN

○ What is the English for dolore?   _____

○ What is the English for morto?   _____

○ What is the English for perso?   _____

○ What is the English for ambulanza?   _____

○ What is the English for telefono?   _____

○ What is the English for fuoco?   _____

○ What is the English for ladro?   _____

○ What is the English for incidente?   _____

○ What is the English for sangue?   _____

○ What is the English for fascia?   _____

TURN BACK FOR THE ANSWERS

○ What is the Italian for pain? _____

○ What is the Italian for dead? _____

○ What is the Italian for lost? _____

○ What is the Italian for ambulance? _____

○ What is the Italian for telephone? _____

○ What is the Italian for fire? _____

○ What is the Italian for thief? _____

○ What is the Italian for accident? _____

○ What is the Italian for blood? _____

○ What is the Italian for bandage? _____

TURN BACK FOR THE ANSWERS

ELEMENTARY GRAMMAR
The word for SOME is DEL.

So,

SOME WINE   is DEL VINO

SOME BREAD is DEL PANE

This is for masculine words.

For feminine words DEL becomes DELLA.

So,

SOME JAM   is DELLA MARMELLATA

SOME BEER is DELLA BIRRA, etc.

For example,

I WANT SOME WINE is VOGLIO DEL VINO

Now cover up the answers below and translate the following:

(You can write your answers in)

1. I WANT SOME RED BLOOD
2. I EAT SOME HARD BREAD
3. HE SEES SOME VERY DIRTY PEPPER
4. SHE WANTS SOME VERY COLD VEAL
5. I HAVE SOME YELLOW BUTTER

The answers are:

1. VOGLIO DEL SANGUE ROSSO
2. MANGIO DEL PANE DURO
3. VEDE DEL PEPE MOLTO SPORCO
4. VUOLE DEL VITELLO MOLTO FREDDO
5. HO DEL BURRO GIALLO

Now cover up the answers below and translate the following:

(You can write your answers in)

1. IL DOLORE E' SULLA COSCIA E NELLA TESTA
2. LA RAGAZZA E' MOLTO MALATA, VUOLE UN DOTTORE
3. IL LADRO HA UNA MANO NERA, TRE COLTELLI VERDI, E SEI FORCHETTE
4. IL FUOCO E' MOLTO CALDO E MOLTO ROSSO
5. L'INCIDENTE E' MOLTO CATTIVO. LA MOGLIE E' MORTA

The answers are:

1. THE PAIN IS ON THE THIGH AND IN THE HEAD
2. THE GIRL IS VERY ILL, SHE WANTS A DOCTOR
3. THE THIEF HAS A BLACK HAND, THREE GREEN KNIVES, AND SIX FORKS
4. THE FIRE IS VERY HOT AND VERY RED
5. THE ACCIDENT IS VERY BAD. THE WIFE IS DEAD

SOME USEFUL WORDS

THINK OF EACH IMAGE IN YOUR MIND'S EYE FOR ABOUT TEN SECONDS

○ The Italian for PLEASE is PER FAVORE   (PAIR FAVORAY)
Imagine saying "POUR FAVOURS, PLEASE."

○ The Italian for THANK YOU is GRAZIE   (GRATSEEAY)
Imagine saying THANK YOU GRACIOUSLY.

○ The Italian for SORRY or EXCUSE ME is MI SCUSI   (MEE SKOOZEE)
Imagine a Chinaman saying "ME EXCUSY, me SORRY."

○ The Italian for HELLO is CIAO   (CHOW)
Imagine saying HELLO to someone who throws CHOW mein at you.

○ The Italian for GOOD NIGHT is BUONA NOTTE   (BWONA NOTTAY)
Imagine putting a bad child to bed and saying "GOOD NIGHT, you have BEEN A NAUGHTY girl."

○ The Italian for IT'S A PLEASURE is PREGO   (PRAYGO)
Imagine telling someone to PRAY GO and he says, "IT'S A PLEASURE."

○ The Italian for HOW DO YOU DO? is PIACERE?   (PYACHAYRAY)
Imagine telling someone "HOW DO YOU DO? — PUT YOUR CHAIR here."

○ The Italian for LEFT is SINISTRO   (SEENEESTRO)
Imagine someone SINISTER who has a LEFT arm covered in blood.

○ The Italian for RIGHT is DESTRO   (DESTRO)
Imagine a Communist saying "I will DESTROY all of the people on the political RIGHT."

○ The Italian for TOWN CENTRE is CENTRO   (CHENTRO)
Imagine the town CENTRE covered in spaghetti.

YOU CAN WRITE YOUR ANSWERS IN

○ What is the English for centro?   ————————

○ What is the English for destro?   ————————

○ What is the English for sinistro?   ————————

○ What is the English for piacere?   ————————

○ What is the English for prego?   ————————

○ What is the English for buona notte?   ————————

○ What is the English for ciao?   ————————

○ What is the English for mi scusi?   ————————

○ What is the English for grazie?   ————————

○ What is the English for per favore?   ————————

TURN BACK FOR THE ANSWERS

COVER UP THE LEFT HAND PAGE BEFORE ANSWERING

○ What is the Italian for town centre? _____

○ What is the Italian for right? _____

○ What is the Italian for left? _____

○ What is the Italian for how do you do? _____

○ What is the Italian for it's a pleasure? _____

○ What is the Italian for good night? _____

○ What is the Italian for hallo? _____

○ What is the Italian for sorry? _____

○ What is the Italian for thank you? _____

○ What is the Italian for please? _____

TURN BACK FOR THE ANSWERS

ELEMENTARY GRAMMAR

In the last section you saw how to use the word for SOME (DEL/DELLA).

When the noun is plural, for example, SOME DOGS, SOME CHICKENS, etc., then the word for SOME is DEI (pronounced like DAY).

So,

SOME DOGS   is DEI CANI

SOME CHICKENS is DEI POLLI, etc.

For feminine nouns the word for SOME is DELLE.

For example,

SOME LEGS   is DELLE GAMBE

SOME HEADS is DELLE TESTE, etc.

For example,

I SEE SOME LEGS is VEDO DELLE GAMBE

Now cover up the answers below and translate the following:

(You can write your answers in)

1. THE HUSBAND HAS A BANDAGE, AND THE DOCTOR HAS SOME BLOOD IN A CUP

2. THE DOG HAS A SMALL FOOT, A DIRTY BACK, A BROWN LEG AND EATS SOME CARROTS

3. THE HEAD AND THE HEART ARE VERY COLD, BUT THE SKIN AND THE BLOOD ARE VERY HOT

4. "I WANT SOME TELEPHONES IN THE ROOM, PLEASE" — "IT'S A PLEASURE"

5. THE AMBULANCE IS LOST, THE WIFE IS DEAD, AT THE TOWN CENTRE

The answers are:

1. IL MARITO HA UNA FASCIA, E IL DOTTORE HA DEL SANGUE IN UNA TAZZA

2. IL CANE HA UN PIEDE PICCOLO, UN DORSO SPORCO, UNA GAMBA MARRONE, E MANGIA DELLE CAROTE

3. LA TESTA E IL CUORE SONO MOLTO FREDDI, MA LA PELLE E IL SANGUE SONO MOLTO CALDI

4. "VOGLIO DEI TELEFONI NELLA STANZA, PER FAVORE" — "PREGO"

5. L'AMBULANZA E' PERSA, LA MOGLIE E' MORTA, AL CENTRO

Now cover up the answers below and translate the following:

(You can write your answers in)

1. CIAO, VOGLIO DEI POLLI
2. LA GAMBA SINISTRA E LA GAMBA DESTRA SONO NEL MARE
3. GRAZIE E BUONA NOTTE, SONO MOLTO STANCO
4. MI SCUSI, MA VOGLIO IL TELEFONO, PER FAVORE
5. PIACERE, SONO MOLTO BRUTTO

The answers are:

1. HELLO, I WANT SOME CHICKENS
2. THE LEFT LEG AND THE RIGHT LEG ARE IN THE SEA
3. THANK YOU AND GOOD NIGHT, I AM VERY TIRED
4. EXCUSE ME, BUT I WANT THE TELEPHONE, PLEASE
5. HOW DO YOU DO, I AM VERY UGLY

MONTHS

The months in Italian are quite similar in sound to the months in English, so no images will be given.

The Italian for JANUARY is GENNAIO

(pronounced JENN Y O — the "Y" is pronounced like the "y" in "mY")

ENGLISH	ITALIAN	PRONOUNCED
January	gennaio	JENN Y O
February	febbraio	FEBR Y O
March	marzo	MARTSO
April	aprile	APREELAY
May	maggio	MAJJO
June	giugno	JUNYO
July	luglio	LOOLYO
August	agosto	AGOSTO
September	settembre	SETTEMBRAY
October	ottobre	OTTOBRAY
November	novembre	NOVEMBRAY
December	dicembre	DEECHEMBRAY

Now cover up the answers below and translate the following:

(You can write your answers in)

1. IN JANUARY, FEBRUARY AND MARCH I DRINK THE RED WINE

2. IN APRIL, MAY AND JUNE THE SAND IS HOT

3. IN JULY, AUGUST AND SEPTEMBER THE WATER IS VERY DIRTY

4. IN OCTOBER, NOVEMBER AND DECEMBER THE DOGS ARE QUIET

5. IN JANUARY, APRIL AND SEPTEMBER THE BULLS EAT THE FLOWERS

The answers are:

1. IN GENNAIO, FEBBRAIO E MARZO BEVO IL VINO ROSSO

2. IN APRILE, MAGGIO E GIUGNO LA SABBIA E' CALDA

3. IN LUGLIO, AGOSTO E SETTEMBRE L'ACQUA E' MOLTO SPORCA

4. IN OTTOBRE, NOVEMBRE E DICEMBRE I CANI SONO TRANQUILLI

5. IN GENNAIO, APRILE E SETTEMBRE I TORI MANGIANO I FIORI

This is the end of the course. We hope you have enjoyed it! Of course words and grammar will not be remembered for ever without revision, but if you look at the book from time to time, you will be surprised at how quickly everything comes back.

When you go abroad, do not be too shy to try out what you have learned. Your host will appreciate your making the effort to speak, even if you are sometimes wrong. And the more you attempt to speak the more you will learn!

GLOSSARY

a	un, una, un'	cabbage	il cavolo
accident	l'incidente	cake	la torta
always	sempre	car	la macchina
am	sono	carpet	il tappeto
ambulance	l'ambulanza	carrot	la carota
and	e	cash desk	la cassa
apple	la mela	castle	il castello
are (they)	sono	cat	il gatto
at	a	caterpillar	il bruco
back	il dorso	chair	la sedia
bad	cattivo	cheque	l'assegno
bandage	la fascia	chicken	il pollo
bank	la banca	church	la chiesa
bathroom	il bagno	clean	pulito
battery	la batteria	cloakroom	la guardaroba
bay	la baia	coffee	il caffè
bear	l'orso	cold	freddo
bed	il letto	countryside	la campagna
bedroom	la camera	cow	la mucca
bee	l'ape (fem.)	cup	la tazza
bill	il conto	cupboard	l'armadio
bird	l'uccello	curtain	la tenda
black	nero	cushion	il cuscino
blood	il sangue	customs	la dogana
blouse	la blusa	danger	il pericolo
blue	blu	daughter	la figlia
boat	il battello	day	il giorno
bonnet	il cofano	dead	morto
book	il libro	deep	profondo
boss	il padrone	dentist	il dentista
boy	il ragazzo	dirty	sporco
brake	il freno	doctor	il dottore
bread	il pane	dog	il cane
breakdown	il guasto	donkey	l'asino
bridge	il ponte	door	la porta
brother	il fratello	drawer	il cassetto
brown	marrone	dress	il vestito
bucket	la secchia	drink (I)	bevo
bull	il toro	drink (they)	bevono
but	ma	drinks (he/she)	beve
butter	il burro	driver	l'autista
butterfly	la farfalla	duck	l'anitra
button	il bottone	eat (I)	mangio

eat (they)	mangiano	have (I)	ho
eats (he/she)	mangia	have (they)	hanno
eggs	le uova	head	la testa
elastic	l'elastico	heart	il cuore
empty	vuoto	heavy	pesante
entrance	l'entrata	help	l'aiuto
envelope	la busta	here	qui
every	ogni	high	alto
excursion	la gita	holidays	le vacanze
exit	l'uscita	horse	il cavallo
expensive	caro	hospital	l'ospedale
factory	la fabbrica	hot	caldo
father	il padre	hour	l'ora
fire	il fuoco	how do you do	piacere
firm	la ditta	how much	quanto
first	primo	husband	il marito
fish	il pesce	in	in
floor	il pavimento	insect	l'insetto
flower	il fiore	is	è
fly	la mosca	it's a pleasure	prego
foot	il piede	jack	il cricco
fork	la forchetta	jacket	la giacca
fresh	fresco	jam	la marmellata
frog	la rana	jellyfish	la medusa
from	da	kitchen	la cucina
fruit	la frutta	knife	il coltello
full	pieno	lake	il lago
game	il giuoco	lamb	l'agnello
garage	il garage	last	ultimo
garden	il giardino	lawyer	l'avvocato
garlic	l'aglio	left	sinistro
girl	la ragazza	leg	la gamba
glass	il bicchiere	lemonade	la limonata
goat	la capra	less	meno
golden	d'oro	letter	la lettera
good night	buona notte	lost	perso
goods	la merce	low	basso
goose	l'oca	manager	il direttore
grass	l'erba	map	la mappa
green	verde	market	il mercato
grey	grigio	meat	la carne
half	mezzo	melon	il melone
hallo	ciao	menu	il menu
hand	la mano	midday	il mezzogiorno
hard	duro	midnight	la mezzanotte
has (he/she)	ha	milk	il latte
hat	il cappello	minute	il minuto

mirror	lo specchio	puts (he/she)	mette
mistake	l'errore	quarter	quarto
money	il danaro	quick	rapido
money exchange	il cambio	quiet	tranquillo
		rat	il topo
month	il mese	red	rosso
more	più	restaurant	il ristorante
morning	la mattina	right	destro
mosquito	la zanzara	river	il fiume
mother	la madre	roof	il tetto
mountain	la montagna	room	la stanza
museum	il museo	salary	il salario
mushroom	il fungo	salt	il sale
narrow	stretto	sand	la sabbia
newspaper	il giornale	sea	il mare
night	la notte	second (adj)	secondo
no	no	second (noun)	il secondo
not	non	secretary	la segretaria
now	adesso	see (I)	vedo
of	di	see (they)	vedono
office	l'ufficio	sees (he/she)	vede
oil	l'olio	sell (I)	vendo
omelette	la frittata	sell (they)	vendono
on	su	sells (he/she)	vende
onion	la cipolla	sheep	la pecora
only	solo	shirt	la camicia
or	o	shoe	la scarpa
owner	il proprietario	shop	il negozio
oyster	l'ostrica	shop assistant	la commessa
pain	il dolore	sick	malato
passport	il passaporto	silver	argenteo
path	il sentiero	sister	la sorella
pear	la pera	skin	la pelle
pepper	il pepe	skirt	la gonna
petrol	la benzina	slow	lento
piano	il pianoforte	small	piccolo
picnic	il picnic	son	il figlio
pig	il porco	soon	presto
plant	la pianta	sorry	mi scusi
plate	il piatto	soup	la minestra
please	per favore	sparking plug	la candela
policeman	il poliziotto	speak (I)	parlo
potato	la patata	speak (they)	parlano
price	il prezzo	speaks (he/she)	parla
product	il prodotto	spoon	il cucchiaio
put (I)	metto	staircase	la scala
put (they)	mettono	stamp	il francobollo

station	la stazione	tyre	la gomma
steak	la bistecca	ugly	brutto
steering wheel	il volante	veal	il vitello
stomach	lo stomaco	very	molto
street	la strada	waiter	il cameriere
sun	il sole	want (I)	voglio
table	la tavola	want (they)	vogliono
tea	il tè	wants (he/she)	vuole
telephone	il telefone	wasp	la vespa
thank you	grazie	water	l'acqua
the	il, la, l', lo, i, gli, le	week	la settimana
		what	che
there	lì	wheel	la ruota
thief	il ladro	where	dove
thigh	la coscia	which	quale
ticket	il biglietto	white	bianco
time	il tempo	who	chi
tired	stanco	why	perchè
to	a	wide	largo
toilet	il gabinetto	wife	la moglie
tomato	il pomodoro	window	la finestra
tomorrow	domani	wine	il vino
town centre	il centro	work	il lavoro
traffic lights	il semaforo	worker	l'operaio
train	il treno	worm	il verme
tree	l'albero	year	l'anno
trousers	i pantaloni	yellow	giallo
trout	la trota	yes	sì

Days of the Week

Sunday	domenica
Monday	lunedì
Tuesday	martedì
Wednesday	mercoledì
Thursday	giovedì
Friday	venerdì
Saturday	sabato

Months of the Year

January	gennaio
February	febbraio
March	marzo
April	aprile
May	maggio
June	giugno
July	luglio
August	agosto

September	settembre	four	quattro
October	ottobre	five	cinque
November	novembre	six	sei
December	dicembre	seven	sette
		eight	otto
Numbers		nine	nove
zero	zero	ten	dieci
one	uno	eleven	undici
two	due	twenty	venti
three	tre	twenty-five	venticinque

LINKWORD ON COMPUTER

First Courses
*FRENCH *GERMAN *SPANISH *ITALIAN
*GREEK *RUSSIAN *DUTCH *PORTUGUESE

On IBM PC & COMPATIBLES, APPLE II Series and BBC Model (B) disk only.
*Also available on MACINTOSH and COMMODORE 64 (USA only).

"O" LEVEL FRENCH

An extensive vocabulary and grammar up to "O" level standard, ideal as a follow-up course to the book or first course programs or as a revision or "brush-up" course for the rusty!

Available on IBM PC & Compatibles; Apricot and Amstrad PCW;

B.B.C. Model (B)

Follow-up courses
*FRENCH *GERMAN *SPANISH *ITALIAN

These courses are ideal follow-up courses for the book or first course computer programmes. They give a further vocabulary and basic grammar.

Available on Disk only.

All courses available from

U.K.	U.S.A.
ACTION COMPUTER SUPPLIES LTD., FREEPOST, WEMBLEY, MIDDLESEX.	ARTWORX INC., 1844 PENFIELD ROAD, PENFIELD, NEW YORK.
TEL: 0800 333333 (FREE)	TEL: (716) 385 6120

LINKWORD,
41 WALTER ROAD,
SWANSEA.

Audio Tape

An audio tape is available as an extra learning aid to accompany this book.

It allows you to hear and to practise the correct pronunciation for all the words used on this course.

Please send a cheque or postal order for £5.95 to

Transworld Readers' Service, 61—63 Uxbridge Road,
Ealing, London W5 5SA

stating which language tape(s) you require and quoting the appropriate number(s) below. All cheques and postal orders must be in £ sterling and made payable to Transworld Publishers Ltd. The above price includes postage and packaging.
Overseas Customers:
All orders, add £1.50

0552 13225 X   French
0552 13226 8   German
0552 13227 6   Spanish
0552 13228 4   Italian

Name (Block Letters) ....

Address ....

....

Language reference no ....

THE PASTA DIET
by Elisa Celli

THE PASTA DIET is a fantastic diet aimed at the weight-conscious person who loves food and has a hearty appetite. Its secret lies in the fact that while pasta is one of the most nutritious and satisfying of all foods, it is not fattening — one four-ounce helping of pasta equals a mere 155 calories, the same amount as a tiny hamburger.

THE PASTA DIET allows you to eat well with a huge choice of dishes, stay healthy, keep your sanity and, most important of all: lose weight.

Complete day-by-day menus and recipes for a 14-day programme in which you can lose 10 pounds of ugly fat.

Over one hundred terrific recipes for main dishes, dips, sauces, salads, desserts and delicious food for entertaining.

Pasta cooking tips.

Economical — whether you cook yourself or eat out.

An alternative 30-day plan to help you lose weight gradually or to maintain your weight loss.

Simple Italian-style exercises to help you diet more effectively.

Calorie count per serving for every dish.

Pasta dishes are quick and easy to prepare.

THE PASTA DIET — it'll make you enjoy losing weight.

0 552 12816 3 £2.50

FRENCH FOOD À L'ANGLAISE
by Brigitte Tilleray

French Food à L'Anglaise is a superbly practical book which acknowledges the fact that French cooking in Britain often has to differ from strict Gallic tradition to be truly successful in the hands of a British cook.

Brigitte Tilleray, a Frenchwoman from a long line of cooks, has been married to an Englishman for fifteen years, and knows from first-hand experience that her glorious cooking must be tempered with a little bit of caution for the sensitive Anglo-Saxon palate.

She has therefore taken authentic French recipes — many from her own rich heritage — and has silently adapted them without sacrificing their essential qualities or good taste, to present a delicious range of dishes suitable for everyday food and for entertaining and impressing guests. She also passes on sound advice on buying and preparing food, and tips on the art of French cooking.

0 552 99215 1   £3.50

HIDDEN FRANCE
by Richard Binns

Hidden France is for the independent, discerning traveller who recognises the rewarding benefits that accrue when one gets off the beaten track and well away from package holiday traps. This informative guide book allows the reader to savour the sights, sounds and tastes of rural France; its woods, forests, meadows and pastures; its hills and river valleys; its placid streams and roaring torrents; its ancient villages and medieval buildings; and its vast larder of culinary delights.

Richard Binns has chosen 25 areas in France, each in unspoilt country and nominates four recommended hotels in each area. These are all modest, family-owned establishments, one of which will suit any budget, and offer good, solid value to the visitor.

Hidden France shares with its companion volumes the author's abiding affection for, and comprehensive knowledge of, the France most tourists never find.

0 552 99230 5   £3.95

FRANCE À LA CARTE
by Richard Binns

France à la Carte is a unique guide compiled by Richard Binns and based on twenty-five years of travelling in France. Together with **French Leave 3** this book equips a tourist for the most enjoyable and exciting French holiday they have ever experienced.

The guide uses the different treasures of France under themed headings such as 'Historical Milestones Relived', 'Unknown Rivers', 'Pleasures of Nature' and 'Hidden Corners' to lead the traveller to the many different facets that France possesses.

This book is for every lover of France — the young, the not-so-young, the country-lover and sightseer, the sports enthusiast and the museum browser, the walker and the car driver. **France à la Carte** offers them all a rich feast of pleasure and discovery.

0 552 99231 3   £3.95

FRENCH LEAVE 3
by Richard Binns

THE UNIQUE GUIDE THAT PUTS FRANCE IN YOUR
POCKET

French Leave 3, completely revised and enlarged by Richard
Binns, is now available for the first time in paperback.

Critical, some may say controversial, reassessments of
many established reputations are just one aspect of this
lively edition of Richard Binns' bestselling guide to France.

* Illustrated with maps of each region featuring the gastro-
  nomic specialities of each area
* 600 recommended hotels and restaurants including many
  more inexpensive locations
* 2,000-plus menu terms translated
* Index of wines and cheeses
* Translation of road signs
* List of base hotels and suggested itineraries for successful
  sightseeing in 22 regions, fully illustrated with maps
* Printed in two colours for easy reference

What the Travel Writers said about the first edition:

'Informative, discerning . . . excellent motorist's guide to
the hotels, restaurants and cuisine of French by-ways'
Richard Barkley, *Sunday Express*

'As vital a companion as your passport'
Christopher Portway, *Annabel*

'A splendid small pocket guide'   *Sunday Times Magazine*

0 552 99232 1   £4.95

EN ROUTE: THE FRENCH AUTOROUTE GUIDE
by Richard Binns

En Route: The French Autoroute Guide by Richard Binns is invaluable for planning a holiday or business trip in France and essential in an emergency. Over 300 French autoroute exits have been researched and mapped by the author.

The exit maps identify and locate a selection of nearby hotels and restaurants — which will suit all pockets — garages, banks, supermarkets, camping and caravanning sites, chemists, petrol stations, public telephones, post offices, car parks, tourist information offices, hospitals, churches, police stations and general shopping areas. 26 route maps show autoroute exits, adjacent main towns, toll booths, service and rest areas and facilities for the disabled.

* Easy to understand and easy to follow
* Over 10,000 pieces of information
* Feeling unwell? Locate the nearest chemist
* Car in trouble? Locate a selection of garages
* Need money fast? Locate nearest banks
* Cheaper petrol than autoroute service stations? Use off-the-autoroute stations or, better still, big supermarkets
* Hotels, restaurants with bedrooms, camping sites: all easily found without the need to buy a series of expensive large-scale maps

0 552 99234 8   £3.95